ENDORSEMENTS TO COME

Seeking out knowledge and teachings throughout his life, Randy Noland writes a great book compiling all his learnings, eagerly sharing them with his readers, and enabling them to live their best life! Anyone looking for a sign to start regaining control of their lives may want to dive in today.

—Peggy McColl
New York Times Best-Selling Author

You Can! by Randy Noland is an aspirational book meant to help the reader unlock their hidden potential using the tools they already embody. Rooted in the philosophy that people were built the exact same way, Randy coaches the readers and encourages them to seek out a specific set of knowledge and beliefs that he knows will help them succeed in life.

—Judy O'Beirn
CEO & Founder, Hasmark Publishing International

DEDICATION

This book is dedicated to you, the reader,
who has been searching for this information.

HOW THIS BOOK CAME ABOUT
AND ITS PURPOSE:

About 2 years after discovering the information in this book, a thought crossed my mind that said: *I'm going to write a book.* When that thought came to me, I literally stopped and asked myself, "What the heck is that all about?" I had never written a book before, and never had a thought like that before. So, I really wasn't sure what the heck that thought was all about.

Over the past 13 years, that thought of writing a book has popped into my mind and been brought to my attention on numerous occasions.

I have never had any idea of what I was supposed to be writing about, so I just let it ride and take its course knowing in my heart that everything happens for a reason and it will all work its way out.

Then the day came at the beginning of September 2020 when I walked into our business and sat down at the computer. That's when I heard this inner voice say loud and clear: ***TODAY IS THE DAY YOU START WRITING YOUR BOOK!***

At that point, I still had NO IDEA what I was supposed to be writing about.

YOU CAN!

UNLOCK your hidden powers and create the life of YOUR DREAMS…

BY

RANDY J NOLAND

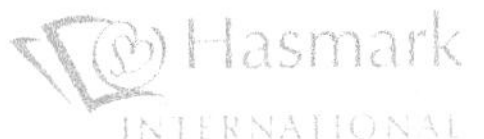

Published by
Hasmark Publishing International
www.hasmarkpublishing.com

Disclaimer:

This book is designed to provide information and motivation to our readers. It is sold with the understanding that the publisher is not engaged to render any type of psychological, legal, or any other kind of professional advice. The content of each article is the sole expression and opinion of its author, and not necessarily that of the publisher. No warranties or guarantees are expressed or implied by the publisher's choice to include any of the content in this volume. Neither the publisher nor the individual author(s) shall be liable for any physical, psychological, emotional, financial, or commercial damages, including, but not limited to, special, incidental, consequential or other damages. Our views and rights are the same: You are responsible for your own choices, actions, and results.

Permission should be addressed in writing to Randy at
yourpath2freedom1@gmail.com

Book Design: Amit Dey
amit@hasmarkpublishing.com

ISBN 13: 978-1-77482-012-4
ISBN 10: 1774820129

Then the craziest thing happened.

I followed my heart, opened my laptop, started with a blank page, and quickly found out that the purpose of the book I would write was to WAKE THE WORLD UP to some things that most people are not aware of. I was supposed to write about what I have learned over the last 15 years, and use some of my personal experiences that have resulted from all of this information so that I can reach out and help as many other people as possible who may be looking to make big changes and great things happen in their lives.

Because of the drastic changes and results that have transpired in my life over the last 15 years from these teachings, principles, and knowledge, it was brought to my attention that I needed to share them with as many people as possible because I know in my heart there are many more people just like myself who are looking for this information; 15 years ago, I was one of them.

Which brings you and me to where we are today.

So hang on and get ready because you are about to embark on a fabulous journey that IS going to change your life forever and teach you how to create **ANYTHING** and **EVERYTHING** you could possibly ever want in your life … **IF YOU** will just **TRUST, BELIEVE,** and **HAVE FAITH** in the information you are about to become aware of.

YOU are about to discover and become aware of some things that ALL of the great leaders of our past have used and applied to make great things happen in their lives.

And guess what? Believe it or not, the vast majority of our population are totally unaware of this information. So I urge you to open your mind and pay very close attention to the information that's to come.

TABLE OF CONTENTS

Chapter 1

SOME WORDS FROM THE AUTHOR

What YOU are holding in your hands right now is nothing short of the most amazing information that you will ever need or want to come into your life, for the rest of your life, as long as you are here on this planet and living in this Universe.

In order for you to receive all that is being offered here, I need to be able to get something straight with you right here and now.

It is NO coincidence that this information has found its way to you. As a matter of fact, that's one of the things that you really need to THINK about and understand.

There are NO coincidences, and EVERYTHING happens for a reason!

You have been looking for this information for a long time, and guess what? It just showed up!

Believe it or not, YOU have brought this information right to yourself probably without even realizing it. You see, *subconsciously,* you've always known that there has to be more to this thing called life, but you have never been taught or took the time to try to figure it out.

So here it is, EVERYTHING you will ever want or need to be able to understand and WIN in this game!

There's been this feeling deep down inside of you for a long time that has been saying there has to be more.

And the good news is that you are right. There is MORE. A LOT MORE!

However, in order for YOU to win in this game called life, you must realize that it's just like any other game you will ever play. You have to understand the RULES OF THE GAME and KNOW HOW TO PLAY IT!

Then you have to practice, practice, practice!

Think about it. YOU can't expect to WIN if you don't know how to play the game.

In every area of your life, there has never been one single moment when you have just jumped in and tried something new and mastered it the first time around.

Well, this is NO different!

What you're holding in your hands are all the RULES and knowledge that have come down from some of the greatest leaders that this world has ever seen.

These leaders are NO different from you and me. The only thing that's different about them is the way they played the game and the RULES they used to win. That's It!

The pages that follow contain ALL the knowledge, proof, and practical methods necessary for accomplishing ANYTHING and EVERYTHING that you could possibly ever want for the rest of your life.

AND YES, I MEAN ANYTHING AND EVERYTHING!
So, stop right now and really try to grasp all that is being offered here.

Please do the biggest favor you could ever do for yourself, and for everyone that you love, and really pay close attention to EVERYTHING that follows.

Unshackle yourself right here and now from the ties that have been holding you back for many years once and for all. Open your mind and unleash all YOUR HIDDEN POWERS that have been locked up inside of you just waiting for you to access them in order to create the life of your dreams.

The information and knowledge, along with examples of how to apply and use them, are all at your fingertips just waiting for you to take hold of them and apply them to your life.

There is nothing wrong with you, so get that out of your mind right now!

YOU are perfect! YOU were brought here for a reason and you are ready to embark on the most amazing journey for yourself … IF YOU will just open yourself up to some things that YOU have NOT previously been aware of.

The information in the following pages has always been available to us. It has been around and used for many years by people just like you and me, but we were never taught it or made aware that it even existed.

I hope you are excited, because you really have something to be excited about!

You have just taken the first step to finally taking control of your life once and for all.

As I already stated, this information has been around for hundreds of years and has been used by some of the most successful people and greatest leaders this world has ever seen or known, so rest assured it is real and it does work.

If you've been wondering how to make this thing called life work for YOU, the answers are all right here. There is NO NEED to look any further.

There is no guessing game here; this is all straightforward information that I can personally guarantee will work for you IF you will just BELIEVE and TRUST in what you are about to find out.

I know this because I found out about it when I was at the lowest point in my life. If I wanted to survive, I had to open myself up and put my trust and belief in someone that I met through a video and follow his lead. That's exactly what I did. I made a decision to bet on myself and give it a chance, and it literally changed my entire world.

There is nothing different about you compared to anyone else who has ever accessed and utilized this information. The ONLY difference is that they understood and applied the information knowing in their hearts that they would get the results they were looking for.

So, lay back and get ready to enjoy this wonderful ride at this point in your life because you are about ready to learn and understand some very important things that the vast majority of our population are not aware of.

Chapter 2

SOME QUESTIONS FOR YOU

Have you ever asked yourself, *is this all there is?*

Have you ever wondered who you really are, and why you are here?

Have you ever said to yourself, *"There has to be more. This can't be all there is."*

Have you ever wondered why things happen in your life the way that they do?

Have you ever asked yourself how do things happen?

Have you ever had images pop into your mind and wondered where they came from?

Have you ever stopped and asked yourself why these images appear, or what they mean?

Have you ever heard voices from within and wondered where the heck they came from, or what they are all about?

Have you ever thought you were crazy when you heard those voices?

Well, the good news is—or maybe I should say the GREAT news is—you ARE NOT crazy!!!!

What we all need to do right here and now is STOP and THINK!!!

Believe it or not, most people really don't THINK.

You might be wondering, *what the heck is this guy talking about? Everybody THINKS.*

But the truth of the matter is, HARDLY anyone thinks!

I used to be one of those people who thought that way too. But it really is so true; most people really don't THINK!

I once heard a guy say that most people can't hold their attention or thought on one subject or idea for more than a few seconds. That would mean that our thoughts are all over the place.

I mean THINK about it for a minute. With all the information going on around us that is coming to us through Radio, TV, Jobs, Family, Internet, and Conversations that are taking place in our presence through people we don't even know.

That Is A Lot Of Information!

If you stop and look around and listen to the conversations that people are having, pay close attention to the things that are coming out of their mouths and the things they are doing. You will quickly realize that this comment I just made about most people not **THINKING** is so true. Because here is a fact: IF they were **THINKING** and paying attention to the things that they were saying and doing, they would never say or do those things in the first place.

You see, the things we **THINK** and talk about are actually creating our realities and our futures. We will get more into that later.

We also need to realize that all these thoughts, questions, images, and voices that are going on in our mind are there for a reason. We may not know why they are there, but they truly are there for a reason. We should stop and **THINK** and be paying attention to those thoughts, questions, images, and voices when they show up. The fact is that up until this point, most of us really don't give them any attention. If we did, things would be different.

All these questions are totally valid. And IF we will be totally honest with ourselves, we all have had times when thoughts, questions, images, and voices have shown up in our lives. Whether we were paying attention to them or not is another story!

I urge you to open your mind and really give some serious consideration to what is being said here.

What you are holding in your hands RIGHT NOW is all the proof and understanding that YOU will ever WANT or NEED to help YOU get right to where YOU WANT to go.

Each and every reader that is receiving this information needs to understand right here and now that there is a reason why this book has found its way to you. My guess is that there is something missing in your life that you truly WANT, and you are still searching for.

The fact that you WANT something is great news. That means that you are still growing.

Another thing I want you to understand is that it does not matter what it is that YOU WANT, the fact that YOU WANT IT is the only prerequisite to it showing up in your life.

And here's my proof that this statement is TRUE.

Somewhere in the neighborhood of 13 years ago I had a thought of writing a book pop into my mind. When that happened, I thought to myself, *what the heck is that all about? I've never written a book before.* I had NO idea what that book was going to be about or when it would come about but as you can see, it has turned into a reality!

And YOU are holding that book in your hands as we speak.

Through this book, my goal and intention are to reach the masses and increase YOUR awareness, along with helping you to understand all the above questions and many more that you may have had in the past.

This information will help YOU to understand who YOU really are and what you are really capable of BEING, DOING, or HAVING in order for you to be able to experience all the beautiful things that your heart desires for the rest of your life!

So, grab onto this information and all the knowledge that is being presented here, and cherish it like it was sent to you straight from GOD. Because it really was!

We have all heard that we have been born with UNLIMITED potential and are capable of doing ANYTHING. However, I think that most of us have either forgotten that fact or just DO NOT BELIEVE IT.

I really THINK this is the case due to everything that is coming at us daily in this world that we live in.

In this day and age, we are moving faster than we ever have because of all the technology that is right at our fingertips. Things are changing at such a fast pace that it is almost impossible to stay caught up.

Just about the time we get accustomed to doing things the way we need to do them, something changes. There is always a new device or technology that's taking the place of something else because it is supposedly better, faster, or whatever the case may be.

YOU simply CANNOT dispute the fact that there is a lot of stuff going on out there today; things come to us from all different angles that grab our attention through the radio, news, jobs, friends, or just random conversations from people we don't even know.

The information, statements, and examples that you are about to indulge yourself in were NOT originated by myself. It is all information that I have listened to, read, studied, or watched someone else teach and explaining over the past 16 years of my life. It all comes from some of the greatest leaders and teachers that this world has ever seen over the last 125 or so years.

You can ensure yourself right now that this is rock-solid information that YOU can use and apply in your life starting today to get the results you really want for the rest of your life.

All the events and experiences that will be listed later in this book are real-life experiences that I have personally experienced over the course of my lifetime. Those events and experiences will justify the fact that YOUR THOUGHTS truly do create your life!

Whether YOU understand and believe that or not, it's true!

There will be many areas in the coming pages that you will want to come back to and read over and over again to ensure that you receive the fullest value that all this knowledge and wisdom has to offer.

From this moment forward, if you are wanting to change ANY area in your life, I urge you to **please do the biggest favor you could ever do for yourself and your family and PAY VERY CLOSE ATTENTION to what's to come!**

Chapter 3

EVERYTHING HAPPENS
FOR A REASON

As I mentioned earlier, one of the first things that I think we ALL need to realize is that EVERYTHING happens for a reason. AND that there are NO coincidences!

At the time of writing, the year is 2020, I am 58 years old, Donald Trump is President, we are about 6 months into the Covid-19 Virus, and in my opinion, most people are running around confused and unsure about everything. They don't know what to do about the virus, and are wondering what is going to happen with the world that we live in. All you hear everyone talking about is this COVID VIRUS and all the negative things that are taking place because of it. Every time you turn on the TV, news, or browse the Internet, there is always someone voicing their opinion and telling everybody what they think should happen or what needs to be done.

Our children are glued to video games, laptops, computers, and cell phones, and would literally not know what to do or how to act if they didn't have those devices. Whatever happened to kids getting on their bicycles and playing outside with their friends?

All of our government officials that run for office are digging and looking for as much dirt they can find on their opponents in order to make them look bad.

If you stop and really take a serious look at everything that's going on out there in the world, it's no wonder people are confused and unsure about everything.

It is really something else out there.

I would venture to say that the vast majority of people are followers who listen to what everyone else is saying and doing instead of stepping up and making decisions for themselves, taking control, and living the life they truly want.

The facts are the facts, and most people are just confused and unsure about almost everything. If you don't think I am right, then stop and listen, and tell me what you see and hear.

I AM NOT ONE OF THEM!

I will be honest and say that I do realize this virus does exist, and I do realize it is a very serious situation, but I also realize that I can NOT do anything about it! Not one thing.

The ONLY thing I can do is try to protect myself from it.

I surely Can NOT change it! And I realize that.

So, I CHOOSE not to spend my time thinking, worrying, or talking about it.

My reasoning behind this decision is because I now realize that I bring to myself whatever I focus my attention on and spend my time thinking about! So I CHOOSE not to spend my time focusing and THINKING about things that are not helping me.

However, it wasn't always that way for me.

If you take a look around and really pay close attention to what you see and hear, you will notice that most people are just floating through life. They do NOT realize that they control EVERYTHING that comes their way. They are following and listening to what everybody else is doing and talking about. They are all talking and spending their time thinking, worrying, and complaining about anything and everything that comes into their life, and treating themselves as victims without ever stopping and THINKING that they just might have all the POWER to be able to change what is coming to them.

During these times I have noticed, and I truly do believe, that there are currently very few people who are focused and dedicated to creating what they want their lives to be like.

There are only maybe 3 people out of 100 who understand that they do have a choice to make a decision and decide where they are going to go.

And here is the funny part, most of those things that the vast majority of those folks are saying, thinking, complaining, and worrying about, they really have no control over. They can't change it! These things are already happening, and they cannot be changed!

The beautiful thing to know and the TRUTH is that we all have a choice, and we all have the ability to make our own decisions! We can go around listening to the news and everything that everyone else is doing and talking about and let all that we see and hear dictate who we are and where we are going, OR we can make a decision for ourselves and believe that we can BE, DO, or HAVE anything and everything that we want in our lives.

It is OUR choice!

VIKTOR E. FRANKL was a Jewish psychiatrist as a prisoner in a concentration camp during the 2nd World War. He said that it was while he was in that camp that he realized that regardless of the physical or mental abuse that he was subjected to, he knew that NO ONE could cause him to THINK ANYTHING that he didn't want to THINK.

HE KNEW THAT HE HAD A CHOICE!

In the worst of possible situations, this man must have been abused both physically and mentally in ways we could never understand or imagine.

But he said that he still had the ability to choose. He knew that NO ONE could cause him to THINK or BELIEVE something that he didn't want to think or believe.

That means that WE also have the ability to choose and make our own decisions.

We have the ability to ACCEPT or REJECT!

YOU have the ability right now to accept what you are reading and learning, or YOU can reject what you are reading and learning. That choice is Yours!

That's really where we want to be THINKING and UNDERSTANDING!

When something happens that we don't understand or like, we have a choice.

We can make the best of it, learn from it, and look for the good in it (because there is good in it somewhere), OR we can let it beat us up, and run around like we don't have any choices and keep letting everybody and everything else that's going on around us in the world control us and our future and keep us stuck right where we are.

So, when something happens that we don't understand or like, one of the big questions that we should be stopping to ask ourselves is this: *if this situation is already happening and I can't change it, WHY would I ever spend my time and energy thinking, talking about, worrying, and complaining about it?*

I am not going to lie to you here … this is going to take a little time to get accustomed to. It is NOT something that you have been practicing so you are going to have to work at it. It has taken me some time and a lot of practice but, now that I have applied this little technique in my life, I have become more relaxed and patient.

When something happens that I wasn't expecting or don't understand, I have learned that it's important to ask myself two questions:

1. Is there anything I can do to change this situation?
2. Is this situation helping me get to where I want to go?

If the answer to both of those questions is NO, then I don't waste any time or energy thinking about it because I know that it is NOT doing me any good!

Believe it or not, most people don't do that. You see, we are all programmed to REACT to situations instead of RESPOND to them. And there is a really big difference between those two.

When you REACT to a situation, that situation has control of YOU!

When you RESPOND to that situation, YOU control it!

In other words, things happen that you have NO control over or don't understand. It might be something that someone says, an event taking place, such as a flat tire, or a comment from someone.

You have a choice right then and there of how you are going to handle and approach the situation. And here's the kicker, you might only have a split second to make that decision on how you're going to handle that situation.

YOU do have the choice and the opportunity to look at that situation and let it take control of you, leaving you to worry, complain, to ramp and rave about it—OR you can look at it and say: *Hmm … that's interesting. I'm not sure why this is happening. I do realize this situation is happening, but I don't have any control over it, and it's definitely NOT taking me where I want to go, so I am NOT going to spend my energy on it because I know it's not helping me in any way.*

When you do that and make that choice, YOU take control of the situation!

When you learn to handle situations in this way, you will probably notice immediately that YOUR blood pressure is going to drop. You become more relaxed, confident, and at peace with yourself because you are now in control.

So why would the vast majority of the people react, worry, talk, and complain about all these different situations taking place in the world, and why do they listen to all the things that everybody else is talking about, worrying, and complaining about?

The Answer Is Actually Very Simple: It Is Because They Are Ignorant!

Please don't get offended here. Being ignorant does not mean that they are dumb, stupid, or anything crazy like that. As a matter of fact, these people are often very smart individuals. Some of them have studied at some of the best universities in the world and have multiple degrees!

Being ignorant just means that the person is NOT AWARE, and that they have not been educated or made aware of certain things.

We are all ignorant about all kinds of different things. There are so many things that each and every one of us is NOT aware of.

Believe me, I totally understand that situation because I used to be ignorant about the way I was THINKING.

I used to be like the vast majority of the population and just go with the flow and didn't really pay much attention to what I was thinking or talking about. I still find myself doing it at times, but I have gotten a lot better at paying attention and understanding, which means I have become more aware! It's like ANYTHING else.

It takes practice. The more you work at it, the better you get!

You see, the real truth is that we only have control over ONE thing—and that thing is OURSELVES!

We Have Control Over What We THINK And What We BELIEVE!

It doesn't matter what anyone else thinks or says! It really doesn't!

It doesn't matter what happened last year, last month, or yesterday. It actually doesn't matter what took place 30 seconds ago, to tell you the truth. That time has passed. It's gone! We can't change it and we surely can't get it back so it doesn't make any sense to talk, worry, complain, or stress about anything that has already happened. It's done!

The only thing that we do have is NOW!

We have NO idea if tomorrow will ever come. We hope that it will, but in all actuality, we are not even in control of that.

If you take a minute and think about what I just said about being ignorant, you will quickly realize just how true that statement really is.

All we can really do is make the best of what we currently have, which is RIGHT NOW, and be the best that we can possibly be, enjoying that we have it!

Let me elaborate on this to ensure that we are on the same page.

If you want someone to do something that they don't want to do, or if someone wants you to do something that you DON'T want to do, there is absolutely no way that they can force you to do it. They can't force you to change the way you think about a situation, and they sure can't change what you believe! You are who you are, and they are who they are.

The choices they make are theirs and the choices you make are yours! The beliefs you have are yours, and the beliefs they have are theirs.

It's not our job to change ANYONE!

So, when I stopped and realized all these basic things which, deep down inside I already knew, I decided that I was going to start doing things a little differently. Knowing in my heart that if I started doing and THINKING about things differently, I was surely going to get different results for myself in my life!

I WAS GOING TO GET THE RESULTS THAT I WANTED!

Chapter 4

PLEASE LET ME EXPLAIN

Back around 1996 or so was the first time I saw a man named Bob Proctor speaking in a video or a tv program. I don't exactly remember what the situation was, but one thing I remember Bob saying clearly, something that stuck in my mind for many years, is that YOUR THOUGHTS BECOME THINGS!

He was talking to his audience, telling them that they could have ANYTHING they wanted. He was up on the stage and was drawing circles and lines on a board and was explaining to the audience that all they needed to do to get the things that they wanted in their lives was to figure out what **they really wanted** and to **use their mind and THINK!**

I was probably about 35 years old at the time. This stuff Bob was talking about was way over my head. I had never heard anyone talk like this before, but to be perfectly honest with you, there was something about Bob's teachings that really caught my curiosity.

At that time, I thought everything was going pretty good in my life, so I really didn't pay any serious attention to what Bob was talking about, and I sure didn't think for one moment about making any changes in the way I was THINKING and looking at things.

But this statement that he made about YOUR THOUGHTS BECOMING THINGS remained in my mind for years.

Fast forward to 2004, I was 44 years old, I had been married for 22 years, and I was being faced with a situation that required me to make a big decision that was ultimately going to change the course of my life forever. Without going into all the details, I made a decision to leave my wife and file for a divorce. Little did I know that when I made that decision, I was going to find myself in a very bad situation; a situation that I had no idea how I was going to get out of. I quickly found myself with nothing more than the clothes on my back, $60.00 in my pocket, and my truck.

I was really scared and had no idea what was going to happen with my life. I felt like my life had been turned upside down, when in all reality it had actually been turned right side up. I just wasn't AWARE of it at that time!

And here's what happened,

One day in late 2005, I turned on my computer. I'm not sure what the situation was or how it all happened, but I found myself watching and listening to another video that Bob Proctor was presenting!!!!

I stopped and thought to myself, *WOW, this is really strange.* But something quickly made me realize that this situation was not a coincidence and that this information was being brought into my life for a reason. I now realize that I actually wanted and needed this information to show up in my life when it did. You see, I was not very happy or satisfied with very much that was happening in my life at that time, and I definitely did not like the position I was finding myself in.

I knew that I deserved better but, I just did NOT know how I was going to make it happen. The only thing I had going for me at that time was this information that Bob was teaching. I had NO idea if the information he was presenting was TRUE or not. But believe me, I was sure hoping that it was TRUE.

At the time, I was basically backed up against the wall with nowhere else to turn. So I made a decision for myself right then and there that I had nothing to lose and everything to gain by taking a chance on myself and listening and paying close attention to the things this man had to say if I really wanted to change certain things in my life.

As I mentioned before, I had never heard anyone talk the way that Bob talked or say the things that he was saying, but for some strange reason he had my undivided attention this time. The things he was talking about and the way that he was explaining them were really making a lot of sense to me, and giving me reassurance that somehow everything was going to be better going forward.

The things I was hearing him talk about just seemed to resonate with me at the time, and God knows I sure needed and wanted things to turn around in my life.

So, I made a decision that I was going to start spending some time reading different little books like *Think and Grow Rich*,

Don't Sweat the Small Stuff, The Laws Of Attraction by Esther and Jerry Hicks, along with watching more videos of Bob Proctor.

Every chance I had, I was finding myself either reading or watching something that was enlightening me in one area or another, and this was ultimately causing me to change the way I looked at things and life.

I just couldn't seem to get enough of the information I was receiving, and all the possibilities that it could bring.

I didn't realize it at the time, but what was actually happening was that I was educating myself in a lot of different areas that I had really never given much attention to. It was all great stuff that NO ONE had ever taught me before.

Up until this point, it had seemed like I had been looking for answers for a long time about a lot of different things. The information Bob was speaking about was able to help me to start understanding things from a different angle.

When I opened myself up to this new way of thinking, I started studying and applying these teachings into my life, and things really started to turn around quickly.

Chapter 5

WE ARE SPIRITUAL BEINGS – WE LIVE IN A PHYSICAL BODY AND ARE PART OF THIS UNIVERSE THAT WE LIVE IN

When I first heard that statement, I wondered what the heck it meant.

Have you ever wondered why you do the things you do, and why you believe the things that you believe?

I urge you to stop right now and open your mind and really THINK about what I am about to say. As a matter of fact, I would recommend that you really pay very close attention to everything that is being said and presented in this book. Please don't just read through it and treat it like it's just another self-help book, because it is really so much more than that.

THIS IS ABOUT YOUR LIFE!

WE only have one life, and I am sure that you want yours to be the best that it can possibly be. Believe me, it can be ANYTHING that you want it to be … IF you really grasp everything on these pages and seriously apply them into your life. If you do, you will experience nothing but great things going forward, and you will be on the road to accomplishing ANYTHING and EVERYTHING that YOU could possibly ever want from here on in.

But here is the deal: YOU are the only one that can do that! I can't do it for you.

Your mom, dad, sister, brother, aunt, uncle, kids, or anyone else can't do it for you. This is YOUR decision and YOURS alone.

Do you know why they can't do it for you? Because they are NOT YOU!

They have NO idea what you are capable of doing or what you want your life to be like.

And believe it or not, they probably don't know what they really want either, so how can they possibly take you where you want to go or help you get there? They can't …

Pay close attention and really THINK about what's being said in the previous statement about being spiritual beings living in a physical body, and being part of this universe that we all live in. I am sure you will see and understand that this statement is so TRUE!

I mean really THINK about it for a minute. It doesn't take a genius to figure this stuff out or understand it, but what it does take is a different understanding of how things work.

Before we ever existed, at some point in time our parents connected, and a seed was planted inside of our mother. I am sure that we all understand that when that seed was planted inside mom, the genes in that seed were those of both mom and dad. And those genes created us and made us who we are today. But what we were NOT aware of at that time was that when the seed was planted, part of those genes in that seed from both mom and Dad had *their* Mom and Dad's genes in it as well. And *their* Mom and Dad's genes, and *their* Mom and Dad's genes, and so on and so on and so on back for generations.

So if we THINK about that for just a minute, that would mean that the seed that was planted inside mom on the day of our conception actually contained genes from hundreds and possibly thousands of years back down through the generations.

That seed, when it was planted, was being fed by the things that mom was eating and drinking. We heard everything that was going on in Mom's life while we were growing inside of her. We experienced the same feelings that Mom had been experiencing for approximately 280 days while we were inside of her. And then, all of a sudden, we were born and became part of this thing called life.

When you THINK about what is being said here, you will quickly realize that we literally have "inherited" genes from our past that go back for hundreds or maybe even thousands of years! This means that we have literally inherited HABITS and BELIEFS from our past that we were not even aware of, and had nothing to do with. These inherited habits and beliefs are combined with the HABITS and BELIEFS that we have acquired since we arrived here in this world.

Those habits and beliefs are called our PARADIGMS. They control our lives! They cause us to do and act and THINK and believe the things that we do.

This may help all of us to understand WHY we believe and do some of the things that we do. A lot of the time, it's not even up to us.

Chapter 6

WE HAVE ALL BEEN PROGRAMMED

Yes, you heard me right. We have literally been programmed, much in the same way as our computers. We have been programmed by everything that we have ever seen, heard, and experienced in our lives and in the lives of all of our ancestors. Parts of our program have been handed down to us without us even knowing it.

The GREAT news is, **All That Can Be Changed**!

Just like when our computer needs to be updated, we too have the ability to create a new program for ourselves, and we can build that program to be exactly what we want it to be, do, or have. We were just never taught or made aware of these things. We have been IGNORANT of all this information. (At least I know I was).

If you really stop and THINK, you will realize that WE ARE SPIRITUAL BEINGS!

We started out as a seed that was planted. That seed was nurtured and given the things it needed in order to develop and grow into this PHYSICAL form that we call the body that we live in.

Our body is our body, just like our name is our name. It's not really who we are.

As a matter of fact, we never really see who we really are, and we never see who anyone else really is either! The bodies that we see are really just PHYSICAL expressions of our spirit. Our body was created from a seed and our name was given to us when we showed up in this world as a PHYSICAL form. Our parents gave us our name, and that's what we are called.

We all live in this UNIVERSE! We are surrounded by planets and stars that are in outer space. There are land, mountains, and rivers that no one can explain how they came to be. This leads us to the fact that there has to be something much bigger and more powerful than we could ever imagine.

We can call it what we want: GOD, ENERGY, SPIRIT, take your choice. But the fact is that whatever it is has been around for a long time, has created everything, and is so much bigger than we are.

I choose to call it GOD! We know that GOD created this world, and we also know that we were created by GOD!

We have always been told that we were created in GOD'S image, and that we are GOD'S highest form of Creation, and that we have unlimited potential.

But, I'm not so sure that the vast majority of people really understand what that means.

Well, the way that I see it and understand it, since we were created in GOD'S image (and I do believe that we were), that must mean that we were born and given the ability to create! Create what, you may ask?

ANYTHING and EVERYTHING that YOU WANT!

Yes, I MEAN ANYTHING and EVERYTHING!!!

You see, our spiritual DNA is PERFECT! We have everything we need inside of us to be able to CREATE exactly what we want. We DON'T need anything to be able to do that. We already have it!

Our problem is we were never taught that we were born with all this POWER and POTENTIAL. Most of us don't believe that we can BE, DO, or have ANYTHING that we want! Therein lies our main problem ... **WE DON'T BELIEVE!**

We have always been told since we were little kids that we should be satisfied with what we have. That's how we were raised. I'm sure that's how our parents were raised as well, but that is just NOT TRUE!

The TRUTH is that we should NEVER be satisfied with what we have. We should be happy with what we have but NOT satisfied. We should always want more! Wanting more is a sign of growth.

GOD gave us the ability to be, do, and have ANYTHING we want, and HE has put everything that we have in this world today here for us to have and enjoy. So that means we can have them IF we want them. Those things wouldn't be available to us if they weren't meant for us to have!

THINK about it. If you look around at everything that is available to us in this world and ask yourself, "HOW did that get here?" the only possible conclusion that you can come to is that someone CREATED it. And you know what? You would be right!

If you take that idea a little further, you will easily realize that in order for it to be CREATED, someone or something had to first THINK about it for it to come into existence and become a reality. Which would mean that EVERYTHING was first originated from a THOUGHT.

Right now, I want you to stop and look around at everything that you see. Then STOP and THINK about what is really being said here.

Back up just a little bit and THINK about being CREATED by GOD. That means that our SPIRITUAL DNA is PERFECT. There is nothing wrong with us! We already have EVERYTHING that we need in order to CREATE ANYTHING that we WANT. WE don't need to find ANYTHING else … we already have it!

WE ARE PERFECT!

ALL the knowledge, wisdom, tools, resources, and ANYTHING else we need are available to us right here and now.

Deep down inside we all know this to be true.

You see, just like other animals and creatures on this planet, we were all born with five physical senses. We have the ability to SEE, HEAR, SMELL, TASTE, and TOUCH.

From the day we first showed up in this world and up until now, we have been going through our lives letting what we can SEE, HEAR, SMELL, TASTE, and TOUCH dictate what's possible for us. We have all been taught to use those five physical senses to the best of our abilities just like any other muscle we were born with.

And because we have all been ignorant to anything beyond, we have based all the decisions we have made for ourselves on those five physical senses. Which means that we have all limited the results that are possible for us!

It's not our fault! We were never taught anything different and no one has ever taken the time to sit us down and educate us on anything other than that.

There we are being IGNORANT again!

We were NEVER taught the TRUTH! And the TRUTH is that we are PERFECT!

I believe the reason we are all unaware is that 95% of the population are not AWARE of anything except what we have all been taught to believe and understand.

It's like we have been stuck in a prison without even knowing we were in prison in the first place! We have been caged up and limited by our own thoughts and beliefs, along with everyone else's thoughts and beliefs that we have chosen to listen to.

But guess what? I have some really GREAT news for each and every one of you that will benefit you BIG TIME from this day forward … IF you will just open yourself up and THINK!

Chapter 7

WE HAVE SOME AWESOME TOOLS AVAILABLE TO US THAT WE WERE NEVER TAUGHT TO USE

Yes, you did hear me right!

When we were born, we were not only born with the ability to SEE, HEAR, SMELL, TASTE, and TOUCH, like all the other creatures on this planet. We were also born with SOME HIGHER FACULTIES that most of us are not aware of how to use.

I do believe we all know that we have these faculties, but we were never taught how valuable they were to us, and we were surely never taught the proper way to use them to benefit us in our lives.

All other animals and creatures on this planet do not have these faculties.

I believe these higher faculties are what separates us from all the other animals in the animal kingdom, and this is the TRUE meaning behind the sayings that we have heard: we are

CREATED IN GOD'S IMAGE, and we are GOD'S HIGHEST FORM OF CREATION!

Now let's go through these higher faculties and get a quick understanding of what they are, then we will look at how we can use them to benefit our lives.

They are: **PERCEPTION, REASON, INTUITION, MEMORY, WILL, and IMAGINATION.**

Perception – Gives us the ability to look at things in the way that we want to look at them.

Reason – Is why we want things.

Intuition – Is what gives us the ability to pick up on vibrations, put them in our mind, and read them.

Memory – Gives us the ability to look back at previous parts of our lives. (Most people don't realize that we can also plant future memories in our minds.)

Will – Gives us our POWER and ABILITY to focus our attention on a picture or subject on the screen of our mind.

Imagination – Gives us the ABILITY to build beautiful pictures in our minds. We can then take those pictures and Create Ideas of exactly what we want our lives to be like.

THESE PICTURES AND IDEAS ARE NOT MERE FANTASIES!

You can think of these Higher Faculties as muscles. They work just like anything else; once you learn how to use them properly and practice using them, they become stronger and stronger and ultimately are the best tools we have at our disposal.

It is really a shame that we were never properly taught how to use these fantastic tools that we were ALL given to use to benefit us in our lives, and help us to create ANYTHING AND EVERYTHING we could possibly imagine for ourselves.

But The Beautiful Thing Is:

WE CAN NOW!!!!

Wayne Dyer once said, "When you change the way you look at something, that thing you look at begins to change!" (He was talking about using our perception when he made that statement.)

When President Kennedy asked Dr. Warner Von Braun how we could build a spaceship and take it to the moon and bring it back home safely, Dr. Von Braun answered him in 5 simple words: "THE WILL TO DO IT!"

This country and President Kennedy did go on to building that spaceship, and we did return it safely home from the moon!

Napoleon Hill said the "Imagination" is the most MARVELOUS, MIRACULOUS, INCONCEIVABLY powerful force that the world has ever known!

He also said, "Whatever the mind of man can conceive and believe, IT CAN ACHIEVE!"

If you do your homework and some research, you will find that EVERY great leader that we have ever heard from has all agreed on ONE THING. They disagreed on almost everything else, but the one thing that they all were in complete and unanimous agreement on is that **WE BECOME WHAT WE THINK ABOUT!**

This is really HUGE information to each and every one of us, *IF* we will just open ourselves up to the possibilities that it brings.

Heck … THINK about it for a minute. The Wright brothers were a couple of bicycle mechanics from Dayton Ohio that had a vision of flying. The Government had spent millions of dollars trying to get something off the ground, but were unsuccessful. They had come to the conclusion that anything heavier than air would fall straight to the ground.

The Wright brothers' father was a bishop that said they would burn in hell just for THINKING they could fly. But guess what? They didn't care! They had the vision of flying and were determined to make it happen. They did NOT know how, when, or where, but they knew it would happen.

We all know that they did get that man-made airplane off the ground. They didn't just get it off the ground, they actually kept it in the air for 14 seconds!

I mean come on, we are talking about 2 guys with nothing but a vision of flying. Everybody thought they were totally out of their minds, but when it was all said and done, they changed the entire world and the way that we travel with their vision.

They opened people's minds and made them realize that we could fly, and the rest is history!

Thomas Edison was sent home from school one day with a note to his mother. The note stated that young Master Edison was NOT smart enough to attend school and that they didn't want him to come back.

When his mother read that note she decided to tell Thomas that the note said he was too SMART for the school, and they didn't have anyone at the school to teach him further.

So, because of how his mother handled that situation, she changed how Thomas thought about himself. This gave him the confidence that he needed and deserved. He went on to make GREAT things happen. And it all started because of how his mother chose to turn a negative situation into a positive one!

He is the reason we have light today!

I want to make sure that you understand what has been said up to this point.

This is NO JOKE!

This is about YOUR life. If your life is not what you want it to be, YOU have the ability to reach down inside and take a good look at yourself and make a decision for yourself to CREATE ANYTHING that you want for the rest of YOUR life!

YOU DO NOT have to listen or agree with ANYTHING or ANYONE that you don't want to. Remember you can THINK what you want and BELIEVE what you want. YOU HAVE A CHOICE!

Chapter 8

IF YOU KEEP DOING WHAT YOU HAVE BEEN DOING, YOU WILL KEEP GETTING WHAT YOU HAVE BEEN GETTING

You have to realize and understand that in order to create what you want in your life, you cannot continue to do the things you've always done and believe in things the way you have in the past.

Also, I want to let you know that you have to realize that there are NOT going to be a lot of people that you can talk to about this. The masses are unaware and ignorant of this information. YOU must realize that the same was true for all our past leaders at one time, but they didn't care. They overcame those obstacles and created what they wanted. **And YOU can too!**

They were born with the same tools that you were born with. They are NOT any different from YOU. The ONLY thing that was different about them was that they used their minds and their higher faculties to make big things happen in their lives. Things that they **believed** in. They understood that they had unlimited potential, and would not let anyone or anything stand in the way of what they saw and BELIEVED in their minds. They understood that **IF THEY COULD SEE IT IN THEIR MIND, THEY COULD HOLD IT IN THEIR HAND!**

They realized that they did NOT need to know HOW or WHEN it was going to happen. They only **knew** that **they could** and that **it would** materialize and become a reality because they understood the process.

They all exercised an enormous amount of faith to accomplish their dreams. **This means that YOU have to do the same!**

In order to be able to do that you have to first understand what FAITH really means.

If you ask anybody *IF* they have faith. I'm sure they would all say that they do. But when the first thing happens that they don't understand or don't like, it causes them to lose that Faith, and it flies right out the window.

I once heard the best definition of faith that I had ever heard in my life. When I heard it, I got so excited by the definition that I decided to engrave it on the front of my mind and NEVER let it get away from me!

That definition of FAITH is a 3-step process that went like this …

1. FAITH is the ABILITY to SEE the INVISIBLE! (SEE IN YOUR MIND WHAT NO ONE ELSE CAN SEE)

2. BELIEVE in THE INCREDIBLE! (BELIEVE THAT THERE IS SOMETHING MUCH BIGGER THAN YOU THAT GIVES YOU EVERYTHING YOU ASK FOR)

3. THIS ALLOWS US to RECEIVE what the MASSES say is IMPOSSIBLE!

I know that we covered this previously, but I believe it deserves as much attention and consideration as we can possibly give it! I don't think we give it anywhere near as much attention as it deserves.

Just use your wonderful MIND and THINK!

All you have to do is STOP and look around at some of the beautiful things that we have in this world that really have NO explanation of **HOW** they came into existence here on this planet.

Then ask yourself, *HOW?*

When you do that, something inside should ensure you that there has to be SOMETHING way bigger than we are.

Chapter 9

THERE ARE LAWS IN THIS UNIVERSE THAT MOST ARE NOT AWARE OF! THESE ARE NOT MAN-MADE LAWS, AND THEREFORE CAN'T BE CHANGED BY MAN!

When YOU understand what this means and start utilizing these LAWS to your advantage, YOUR world will begin to change and become exactly what you want it to be!

I think it was back around 2006 or 2007 … you may remember that there was a big movement taking place throughout the world that was brought about by a lady that created a movie called **THE SECRET**.

That movie was actually based on a UNIVERSAL LAW called the LAW OF ATTRACTION!

In that movie, they talked a lot about the Law Of Attraction, but they did not really TEACH it!

The LAW OF ATTRACTION is actually a secondary law!

The **LAW OF VIBRATION** is actually the primary law. **THAT LAW STATES THAT EVERYTHING VIBRATES ON ITS OWN FREQUENCY!**

EVERYTHING moves and NOTHING Stands Still!

In order for you to really understand this information, I want you to really STRETCH and THINK!

EVERYTHING that we see with our naked eye is actually moving! It only appears to be standing still. If you were to look at each one of those things under a particular type of microscope you would see that they are ALL moving and VIBRATING. And they are ALL Vibrating at a high speed.

If you go to a scientist and ask them about the vibrations of everything in our Universe, they will tell you that it is CORRECT!

EVERYTHING VIBRATES AND MOVES at its own speed!

A really easy way to understand this is for you to take a look at your phone. Your phone has its OWN number (which is a frequency). Nobody has the same phone number that we have, which means that we all have our own frequency with that phone.

If I have YOUR number on MY phone, I can dial your number and instantly be connected to YOU because I have your number and am on YOUR frequency. I can send you a picture, I can text YOU, and you will get my message instantaneously because I am on YOUR frequency and sent it to YOU!

We all know that if I dial my brother's number, I WON'T get YOU. I will get my BROTHER because I got on his frequency and dialed his number.

So, if you THINK about what is being said here about frequencies, I'm sure that we all can understand.

Let's take that a step further. If what I'm saying is TRUE, and I believe that we will all agree, when we are looking at the example of our phones, that has to mean that EVERYONE who has their own phone has their own frequency and can be contacted through that phone by ANYONE who has that number and chooses to dial it.

So here's the deal. Are you ready?

EVERYTHING that we want is ALREADY HERE!

We DON'T have to get ANYTHING! IT IS ALREADY HERE!

EVERYTHING In This Entire UNIVERSE Operates On Its Own FREQUENCY!

What we have to do is get on the frequency of whatever it is that we want, and stay on it!

When we do that, we begin moving toward whatever it is that we want, and at the same time, those things that we want begin moving toward us.

And I mean EVERYTHING!

You're probably asking yourself right now, *HOW the heck do I get on that frequency of what I want?*

The first thing you need to do is figure out what it is that YOU want. Most people have never really given any serious attention to what it is that they want. I think that's because they really don't **BELIEVE** that they can have what they want.

So they really don't know what they want!

Remember, YOU have unlimited potential, so don't be afraid to really THINK outside the box and stretch. It doesn't matter what anyone else thinks. This is about YOU, and YOU are here to CRE-ATE ANYTHING AND EVERYTHING that YOU want.

What makes this so beautiful is that WE ALL WANT DIF-FERENT THINGS!

And there is an unlimited supply of EVERYTHING here for us here on this planet.

Once we decide exactly what it is that WE WANT in our life and make a COMMITTED DECISION to go after it, this is where the proper use of our **HIGHER FACULTIES** comes into play.

When we UNDERSTAND and BELIEVE that this information is TRUE, we can literally use our **INTUITION** and **IMAGINATION, given to us by GOD**, to attach ourselves to that higher frequency of what it is that we want and use it to build magnificent pictures in our mind of what we want our lives to be like.

We can build it just the way we want it to be. When we do that, we can use another HIGHER FACULTY, which is our **WILL**, and HOLD that picture on the screens of our minds.

When we do that OVER and OVER, we are literally impressing it on our subconscious mind.

Because we have impressed that thought and picture on our subconscious mind repeatedly, and because it is something that we want and enjoy, we will begin to become emotionally involved with that IDEA and THOSE PICTURES.

That is when we become attached to these ideas on an emotional level.

I believe that when that happens, it causes another HIGHER FACULTY to kick in—this is our **PERCEPTION.**

Remember what Wayne Dyer had to say about our PERCEPTION: "WHEN YOU CHANGE THE WAY YOU LOOK AT THINGS, THE THINGS YOU LOOK AT BEGIN TO CHANGE!"

What happens is that our **Perception** of that thing we are seeing in our mind and WANTING begins to change and turns into a DESIRE (which is planted in our heart). We literally fall in love with the idea and our BELIEF in our own ability to achieve it goes way up because we have the KNOWLEDGE and a firm UNDERSTANDING of these LAWS, and because we KNOW that as long as we hold that picture in our mind, **IT WILL MANIFEST IN OUR LIFE!**

IT HAS TO! IT IS THE LAW!

I am sure we have all heard of these simple little sayings written in the bible:

BELIEVE AND YOU SHALL RECEIVE!

ASK AND IT IS GIVEN!

Now really THINK about what those two simple statements, which have been written in the bible and have been around for centuries, really mean. They exist for YOU!

Please do yourself a BIG favor and **BELIEVE!**

I said it before, and I am going to say it again: I really think that's our BIGGEST problem.

WE DON'T BELIEVE!

We say that we BELIEVE, and we want to BELIEVE, but the fact is that most of us are so caught up in all the crazy stuff that's going on around us that we really don't take the time to figure out and understand WHO we really are and what we really want.

Well, I'm here to tell you—and I am not trying to be harsh here but—IF you don't take the time to figure out WHO you really are and what makes you tick, you are fighting a losing battle.

YOU HAVE TO UNDERSTAND WHO YOU REALLY ARE!

Remember those things called PARADIGMS? Well, they are here to keep you right where you are. They don't want you to change. They will fight you every step of the way until you blow through that wall and move into freedom.

And you can only do that by understanding who you really are and how these LAWS work. (And the only way you can get this understanding is through study).

Those PARADIGMS are still going to try to keep you stuck where you are, but now you have the KNOWLEDGE and UNDERSTANDING to change those PARADIGMS and are able to move on to ALL the GREAT things that your heart desires.

You have made a decision for yourself based on what you know in your heart to be TRUE.

I personally THINK and KNOW that it would be very wise for ANYONE who wants to make great things happen for themselves to spend some time and absorb ALL this information and implement it into their lives starting NOW.

TRUST me, IF you do, the rewards are HUGE!

THE LAW OF PERPETUAL TRANSMUTATION:

Back in 1908, there was a man by the name of Andrew Carnegie who, as a child, migrated to the United States from Scotland with his poor family.

Well, that young boy became the richest man in the world!

Andrew Carnegie (the richest man in the world at the time) once said, **"ANY IDEA HELD IN THE MIND that is either FEARED or REVERED WILL BEGIN AT ONCE TO CLOTHE ITSELF IN THE MOST CONVENIENT AND APPROPRIATE FORM AVAILABLE!"**

He said:

> **ANY IDEA HELD IN THE MIND!**
>
> **Feared OR Revered (Wanted or Not).**
>
> **WILL Begin To Clothe Itself!**
>
> **In the most CONVENIENT and APPROPRI-ATE Form Available!**
>
> **He didn't say MIGHT, MAYBE, or Hopefully. HE SAID WILL!**

We should really give some serious attention to what this man was saying.

I mean **THINK** about it … he was the richest man in the world and he started as a poor boy who migrated here from another country. He obviously figured something out that benefitted himself BIG TIME!

What these words mean to me is that **ANY IDEA** that we **FOCUS** on and **HOLD** on the screen of our mind (whether it is something we want or something we don't want) **WILL** begin to start showing you signs of it coming into your life as a physical form!

That is the LAW OF PERPETUAL TRANSMUTATION!

That LAW STATES: ALL energy that is in motion will **EVENTUALLY** appear in the physical form.

THAT IS A LAW OF THE UNIVERSE!

Whatever you are **THINKING** about and **FOCUSING** on **IS** actually moving into form and is going to show up in your life whether you understand and believe it or not.

This is why it is SO important that we are paying attention to what's going on in our minds. Because what is going on inside is what we are bringing into our lives and is what will show up on the outside!

At the same time, by KNOWING this information, we have the capability of using it to our advantage in CREATING WHAT WE WANT!

AND IT ALL STARTS WITH OUR THOUGHTS!

THE LAW OF GRATITUDE:

Wallace D Wattles wrote a book titled *The Science Of Getting Rich*. The 7th chapter of that book is about GRATITUDE.

He clearly states in the first few lines of that chapter that the first thing we need to do is to convey our idea of what we want to as a formless substance (which is God).

In order to be able to do that, you have to be able to relate yourself to that formless substance in a harmonious way.

I think what he is saying is that we need to be spiritually connected from our heart and have the understanding that we are a part of that formless substance, and that we are connected to it and we should be GRATEFUL for that.

He goes on to say how vitally important it is to have that connection, and that when we do, we will bring ourselves into perfect unity with the mind of God.

He said the entire process of mental adjustment can be summed up in one word: GRATITUDE!

First, **BELIEVE** that there is **ONE** intelligent substance from which **EVERYTHING** is derived.

Second, **BELIEVE** that this substance gives us **EVERYTHING** that we desire.

Third, relate ourselves to it by a feeling of deep and profound GRATITUDE.

I think this is where a lot of people make mistakes. I really don't think most people take the time to be grateful!

I remember when I was like that. But I changed my way of thinking, and GRATITUDE has become a huge part of my life.

Because I understand how important it is to be grateful.

There is a LAW of GRATITUDE, and it is absolutely necessary that you observe that law if you are to get the results you seek.

He says that the Law of Gratitude is a natural principle; action and reaction are ALWAYS equal and in opposite directions.

Reaching out with your MIND in thankful praise is an expenditure of FORCE. That force **CANNOT FAIL** to reach that to which it is addressed.

In other words, **IT MUST COME. IT IS LAW!**

The grateful mind always expects good things, and EXPECTATION becomes FAITH. The reaction of gratitude in one's mind actually produces faith.

It is necessary that we create a habit of being grateful for everything good that comes to us, and we should be giving thanks continuously.

And that is because ALL things have contributed to our advancement, to where we are currently at, and because of that we should be grateful for EVERYTHING!

I urge you to take some time and really THINK about what's being said here and start applying some of your time EVERY DAY to being GRATEFUL for EVERYTHING that you currently have.

I have applied this principle in my life, and it has made such a big difference in my results.

To show you how POWERFUL this law is, the next time you are not feeling up to par or are upset about something, start going over ALL the things you have to be GRATEFUL for in your mind. And Believe me, they are substantial.

For example:

1. The fact that YOU woke up this morning.
2. The fact that YOU have something to eat.
3. The fact that YOU have a place to call home and rest your head at night.
4. The fact that YOU are beautiful.
5. The fact that YOU have the ability to DREAM.
6. The fact that YOU have people in your life who LOVE YOU.

7. The fact that YOU have the opportunity to get it right.

8. The fact that YOU have any form of health.

9. The fact that this information has found its way to YOU.

10. The fact that YOU are GOD'S HIGHEST FORM OF CREATION and have all the POWER to CREATE anything that you want.

11. The fact that you can take a bath and drink clean water.

I could go on and on, which shows you that we really do have so much to be GRATEFUL for, and that we take many things for granted.

When you take time to be grateful, you will notice what a different VIBRATION you are in compared to when you started. It Is amazing!

You should really make GRATITUDE a big part of your life if you expect to receive what you want.

Dr. Joseph Murphy wrote a beautiful book called *The Power Of The Subconscious Mind*.

In that book there is a chapter that says:

"WE HAVE A MIND AND WE SHOULD LEARN HOW TO USE IT!"

He stated that there are actually two levels of our minds—the CONSCIOUS MIND and the SUBCONSCIOUS MIND!

He said that we **THINK** with our CONSCIOUS mind, and whatever we HABITUALLY THINK sinks down into our

SUBCONSCIOUS mind and CREATES according to OUR thoughts! Our SUBCONSCIOUS mind is our CREATIVE mind!

If you think GOOD, GOOD WILL FOLLOW. If you think EVIL, EVIL will follow!

This is the way that OUR minds work.

Your subconscious mind is different from your conscious mind.

Your conscious mind gives you the ability to THINK, reason, build, and CREATE!

Your subconscious mind does not have those abilities. Your subconscious mind MUST ACCEPT ANYTHING that YOU choose to impress on it.

The subconscious mind CANNOT change what is impressed on it. It can ONLY ACCEPT IT!

THIS IS REALLY HUGE to us IF we will ACCEPT it. WE can make big things happen for ourselves just by understanding and applying what is being taught here.

Dr. Murphy said the main point to remember is that once our SUBCONSCIOUS mind accepts an idea, it begins to execute it! The only thing we have to do is get our SUBCONSCIOUS mind to accept the idea! And when we do, the LAW of our SUBCONSCIOUS mind will bring forth the desire that we want.

The LAW of our mind is this: You WILL get a response from YOUR subconscious mind according to the nature of the

THOUGHT or IDEA that you hold in YOUR CONSCIOUS mind!

THINK about it like this:

Your conscious mind is like the captain of a ship. The captain DIRECTS that ship and gives orders to the men on the ship, who in turn control how the ship operates and where it goes. Those men don't know where they are going. THEY FOLLOW ORDERS.

They would end up crashing or sinking, or possibly end up on land, if the CAPTAIN issued them the wrong instructions.

The men obey him because he is in charge and gives the instructions. They automatically obey him. They don't talk back or question the CAPTAIN, they just follow the orders that he issues.

Your CONSCIOUS mind is the CAPTAIN and the MASTER of YOUR ship (which is your body, environment, and all your affairs).

Your SUBCONSCIOUS mind takes the orders that are given by YOUR CONSCIOUS mind based on what it BELIEVES and ACCEPTS as TRUE, and it follows YOUR orders!

Here is another way to THINK about it:

If we want to plant a new garden in our backyard, what is the first thing we have to do?

We have to get the soil prepared, right? This means we have to clean all the weeds, turn the soil, and get it moist and ready for the planting of our seeds.

Once that is done, we get our seeds and poke little holes in the earth and start planting. Then we cover those seeds with the earth.

We know in our HEARTS and our MINDS that we planted those seeds.

So, we come out EVERY DAY and make sure our garden is doing well. We make sure the soil is kept moist and clean, and we keep away anything that does NOT belong there.

We DON'T see anything showing on the surface, but we KNOW that we planted those seeds.

We keep taking care of that garden even though we don't see anything showing on the surface. Because we KNOW we planted those seeds.

The day comes, and we walk outside to take care of the garden and we see little sprouts starting to pop through the surface and show themselves. We DON'T pull them out of the ground, right?

No, because we know that if we keep taking care of them, they will continue to grow. So, we keep taking care of them and watering the garden, and keeping everything clean.

Then the day comes when those seeds harvest! It could be corn, roses, apples, or whatever. I don't care what kind of seeds that we plant or what they are—they all work the same way.

Guess what? **OUR MIND WORKS EXACTLY THE SAME WAY!!!**

Your THOUGHTS are YOUR seeds. When you give those thoughts your attention, you are watering them. They start growing. You don't see them growing, but they are. Then the day comes, and you start seeing some EVIDENCE of those seeds growing. You keep giving them attention, and guess what happens?

THEY HARVEST!!!!

Those THOUGHT seeds are SPIRITUAL SEEDS. We DON'T KNOW HOW LONG THEY ARE GOING TO TAKE TO HARVEST. All that we know is that **THEY WILL!**

This is how it all works.

We have always heard that we have UNLIMITED potential, but I honestly believe that most of us don't understand what that really means.

To me, it means exactly what it says. WE ARE UNLIMITED! That we can BE, do, and have ANYTHING and EVERY-THING that we want IF we will just get with the program and change what we have been taught and handed down.

The fact is that we have to change the way we THINK!

We have to open ourselves up to the possibilities that this information just might be true. Because it is TRUE, whether you believe that it is or not.

And by the way, the only reason you would think that this information is not true at this point is because of YOUR PRO-GRAM (which is your paradigm).

When we buy into this information and start applying it to our lives with the understanding that we don't care what anyone else thinks or says about what we BELIEVE and UNDERSTAND, we open ourselves up to nothing but great things happening in our lives.

Why? Because that's what WE decided that WE WANTED.

Also, it does NOT take any more effort to reach and stretch for something that you consider to be BIG than it does to reach and stretch for something that you consider to be small. It all takes the same amount of effort, so why wouldn't we go for the BIG stuff that we want?

I will tell you now that it takes discipline, belief, courage, faith, knowledge, and understanding to make this change, because everyone from your outside world is going to think you're crazy. They might even laugh at you. This is why you have to be careful about who you share this information with. Remember, 95% of the population is totally unaware and ignorant of all of this!

You have to be willing to hold your ground and continue moving and believing in what you can see in your mind, and know in your heart that it is there for a reason and that it belongs to YOU.

You have to understand that it is really an inside job. Everything that's going on in the inside HAS to show itself on the outside.

THAT IS A UNIVERSAL LAW!

When you do that, you are demonstrating faith and believing what YOU can see in your mind. Remember, NO ONE can see what you see.

The fact that YOU can see it in YOUR mind should be all the proof that you would ever need to help yourself understand that it is there for a reason, waiting for YOU.

HABAKKUK 2:2-3, a scripture from the bible, says:

"WRITE THE VISION AND MAKE IT PLAIN!

SO THAT HE WHO READS IT WILL RUN TO IT.

EVEN THOUGH IT TARRIES (TAKES SOME TIME)

WAIT FOR IT! BECAUSE SURELY IT WILL COME AT

AN APPOINTED TIME!"

We have to FOCUS our attention on what WE WANT!

We have to use our IMAGINATION to build great pictures in our minds, and hold on to them!

We have to understand that there is something way bigger than us that is ultimately in charge and gives us ANYTHING and EVERYTHING that we have ever asked for.

We have to UNDERSTAND the process, and stand strong BELIEVING in what we know (which is having FAITH).

And we have to be GRATEFUL and give thanks.

Remember, FAITH is the ability to see the INVISIBLE and BELIEVE in the INCREDIBLE!

When we do that, he delivers it right to us WITHOUT FAIL!

WE are the ones who limit ourselves!

We limit ourselves BY OUR WEAKNESS OF ATTENTION AND OUR POVERTY OF IMAGINATION!

That means that we don't spend anywhere near the amount of time needed to FOCUS on WHAT WE WANT, and WE surely don't use our IMAGINATION as much as we should in order to be able to build those pictures and make our dreams come true!

IF YOU CAN SEE IT IN YOUR MIND, YOU CAN HOLD IT IN YOUR HAND!

Chapter 10

HOW I BECAME
A FIREFIGHTER

So, I really started studying seriously and learning all this information back in 2005 right when I was in the midst of all this hell that had broken loose in my life from the divorce that I had initiated the year before.

I stopped and thought about what I was learning. And as I did, I started to look back at my life. The first thing that popped into my mind was a time when I was about 8 or 9 years old.

I remembered clearly a day when I was walking to school by myself.

You see, we lived about a mile or so down the street from the school that I attended. I remember that a loud siren on a fire truck caught my attention. I stopped dead in my tracks to watch the fire truck as it was coming down the street in my direction. I was basically the same as most little boys that age, and was fascinated by the fire truck and the firemen. As they got closer, I remember waving to the firemen as their truck screamed by on the way to whatever emergency they had been called to.

At that point a thought popped into my mind that said, "When I grow up, I want to be a fireman."

I didn't really give it much attention at the time, but I do remember having that thought.

Well, fast forward to when I was about 17 years old getting ready to graduate from high school. I woke up one day and was telling my Dad that I was thinking about going to talk with a recruiter about joining the military. My Dad had been in the Air Force when he was a young man.

He asked me if I had any idea what I would want to do for a job if I joined the military.

At the time, I didn't have any idea what I wanted to do in the military, or in my life for that matter. I wasn't even sure that I was going to enlist at all at the time. All I knew is that I woke up with this idea and all I wanted to do was go talk to someone and see what my options were.

So, that's exactly what I did. I met with a recruiter and talked about my options. He explained that in order for me to find out what jobs I qualified to do in the military, I would have to take a test. So, we started the process and a few days later he drove me into downtown Los Angeles where I was able to take this test to see what jobs I qualified for IF I decided to enlist. I was considering going into the Air Force, but as I said, nothing was cast in stone at that time.

I took the test and was contacted by the recruiter a few days later, and low and behold, he said that according to my test results I could basically choose any career field that I wanted in the Air Force, and that I would be accepted.

So, I thought about it for a few days. That's when this thought came to my mind about becoming a FIREFIGHTER. That SAME THOUGHT that I had when I was watching that fire truck scream by that day had popped back into my mind. When that happened, I made the decision of what I was going to do. I signed the appropriate papers, took my physical, and was set to become a fireman in the USAF. Nine months later in September of 1980, I left for bootcamp.

After completing my bootcamp training I went to a tech school in Illinois, and was later stationed in Okinawa, Japan, for my first assignment as a fireman.

I spent 2 years in Okinawa, then back to the states I came to finish out my 4-year obligation with the USAF.

When the time came in September of 1984, I decided to leave the military. I was discharged honorably.

The main point I want to make here is that when I look back, I can clearly see how the entire situation of becoming a fireman took place, and I could not help but realize that I actually made that happen with my thoughts—the thoughts I had way back when I was just a young boy!

It doesn't matter how I view the situation. I realize that I was the only person who knew in my heart and my mind that this is exactly what happened, and how it all came about.

Chapter 11

MY CAREER AS AN INDUSTRIAL MAINTENANCE MANAGER CAME RIGHT TO ME!

I continued looking back at my past as I was putting this knowledge and information together in my mind, and I remembered a day when I was out in my garage working with my brother-in-law on a car that I was fixing up.

It must have been around 1986 or so. I was pretty good with my hands and with tools, which I found kind of strange because when I was a young boy, my dad was always trying to get me to help him work on things in the garage. At the time, I just had no interest.

My dad was a jack of all trades. There wasn't anything that guy couldn't fix. You name it: cars, radios, TVs—he could fix anything! But I never had any interest in learning these skills or getting involved back when I was younger.

Well, as I grew older, I started noticing that I kind of liked working on cars and motorcycles and basically anything that had an engine. So, there I was in the garage working with my brother-in-law on a little car that I had bought, and all of a sudden, right out of nowhere, he made a comment to me that I should look into becoming an industrial maintenance mechanic. I had no idea what that was.

My brother-in-law was a full-blown industrial maintenance electrician, so he explained to me that these manufacturing facilities had equipment that needed to be repaired from time to time. They needed in-house mechanics to be able to fix the equipment when it broke down. He also told me that those mechanics earned pretty good money, which caught my attention.

I thought to myself, *that's kind of interesting*, but that's about as far as it went.

A few months passed by, and I had landed a job working at a food manufacturing facility as a machine operator. I had probably been working there only about 6 or 8 months when, one day, I looked on the company bulletin board and noticed that they had a job opening for a MAINTENANCE MECHANIC. According to the post, if there was anyone in the facility who thought they should be considered for the position, they should write their name on the board!

I will never forget that day. I was talking to one of the mechanics when I asked if he thought they would be willing to hire someone with NO experience. He said he did not think so, but he told me that the posting was there for anyone who wanted to be considered for the position. I ended up putting my name on the long list, along with many other employees from various departments in the company.

Guess what happened?

I ended up being called up to the maintenance department a few weeks later where I met the Chief Engineer. His name was Vic Holman. (I am sorry to say that he is no longer with us.) Now, I had zero experience and had never worked in that type of environment before, and after talking to Vic for about 30 minutes, I had the feeling that he was really looking for someone who had a lot more experience than I did. I thanked him for his time and the opportunity to meet with him.

I started walking out of the maintenance shop when I heard this voice say, "Hang on, young man." He wanted to talk to me for a few more minutes. Vic had actually gotten up from his desk as I was walking away and had come out to stop me. He asked me a few more quick questions, and I answered him by saying IF you would be willing to give me a chance, I promise you I will do the best I can possibly do, and I will prove myself to you.

That is when he said, "Listen, young man, I really like your attitude and confidence. I want you to report here on Monday morning at 6 am. Can you do that?"

He said he was giving me 30 days to prove my abilities to hold the position.

I walked away from that conversation so happy and excited because I realized that this could be a great opportunity for me to really learn some things that I could possibly take with me for the rest of my life if I chose to make a career in this industry as a mechanic.

I didn't realize it at the time, but this man was ultimately looking for someone who could lead and direct his entire maintenance department staff in getting things done. Little did I know, but the company was actually expanding and preparing to install some new production lines.

Before my 30 days of training was up, Vic had taken a special liking to me, and personally started training and teaching me some little tricks of the trade. In about 8 months' time, I actually ended up leading and directing the entire maintenance crew at that facility.

At some point during my time of being a mechanic at that facility, I remember thinking to myself that I would ultimately like to someday be in the position that Vic was in. He ran the entire show. He made all the decisions for the company from a maintenance standpoint, and was in charge of millions of dollars for the upkeep and growth of the business.

I continued learning and applying myself to become the best I could be at my job. After about 7 years, the day came when the company was sold to another company from back east. I had an opportunity to move with the company, but I chose not to because I had a family that was based in Southern California.

I ended up taking another maintenance position with a different company, but after about 2 years I realized that I wasn't happy doing what I was doing, so I started looking for another opportunity.

I was online one evening when I happened to stroll across an ad for a major food manufacturing operation that had a worldwide presence and great reputation. That facility was supposedly located only a few miles from where I was currently living.

I knew that area very well, but in my mind, I just could not place where that facility was actually located.

I submitted my resume on that Friday night and decided that I was going to get in my car the following day and see if I could find the company's location. Low and behold, I did find the location of the plant. I was blown away because I never knew that it was located there, and it had been there for over 30 years.

I remember pulling into the parking lot when I initially found the place. I stopped and got out of my car, and walked around the entire building checking out whatever I could see from the outside looking through the fence. I was liking what I was seeing.

I got back in my car after about 30 minutes and said to myself, I WOULD REALLY LIKE TO HAVE THAT JOB!

Monday morning, I received a phone call asking if I was available to come in for an interview.

The short story is that I was ultimately hired as the Maintenance Manager for that organization, and I became the person in charge of the entire facility from a maintenance standpoint. I was in charge of millions of dollars in capital spending for the company, and was the person that everyone came to for their maintenance and company growth needs.

Remember, all this happened to a guy that started with absolutely NO experience or knowledge of the industry.

I held that position for about 8 years, then the day came when they decided to relocate the facility. I was asked if I wanted to move with the company, but decided to pass on that opportunity as well.

My maintenance career ultimately lasted until late 2014 when I decided I had enough.

So, it must have been sometime in late 2008, I had been finished with my divorce for about 2 years and had been studying this information seriously during those 2 years. All kinds of great things had been happening in my life, and here I was once again realizing exactly how it had all come into play for me—without ever knowing I was actually causing it to happen.

IT HAD ALL STARTED WITH MY THOUGHTS ONCE AGAIN!

I was totally amazed and fascinated with this information, and how it had begun to work in my life. I was blown away that for all these years I had never known anything about this stuff.

TO THIS DAY, I STILL FIND THIS INFORMATION FASCINATING!

Chapter 12

HOW I BOUGHT MY
2009 CORVETTE

So here I was in late 2008 seeing in my mind how these teachings and knowledge I had gathered had all come into play for me in my life without ever really being AWARE of what I was doing. I decided that I was going to try and apply these teachings "deliberately" this time, and pay close attention to the results.

I had always admired Corvettes for as long as I can remember. A neighbor of mine was always building Hot Rods in his garage from the ground up, and his son had a 1964 Corvette parked in their garage. I used to love to go over and look at that car.

I had never dreamed that I could actually buy and own one personally, but after seeing how these LAWS and the UNIVERSE were working in my life, I made a decision to apply myself toward that goal.

I started looking at Corvettes on the internet, browsing E-bay. I also talked to a friend of mine and was telling him how I wanted to buy one.

These types of things had been going on for about 3 months, when one day I found myself heading to a friend's house for a visit. As I was on my way there, I passed a Chevrolet dealership that had about 7 or 8 brand-new 2009 Corvettes lined up on the front row of the parking lot, which I noticed as I rounded the corner.

I had driven by that dealership many times before, but as I passed the dealership that day, those Corvettes seemed to jump out at me.

As I passed about the 5th Corvette in the line, I found myself pulling my car over to the curb and backing up to where the 1st Corvette was parked. I wasn't even really thinking about what I was doing.

I'm serious. It all happened so fast that I really didn't even have time to think about it. It was like a magnet was pulling me.

I got out of my car and proceeded to walk onto the lot and headed directly up to one particular car. As I walked up, I was really admiring how beautiful it was. It was a candy-orange Corvette with sparkles in it, and IT WAS BEAUTIFUL!

I walked around it very slowly admiring every single line and curve. As I walked around it, I was completely lost for words. As I made it back around to the driver's side, which is where I started, the salesman came walking out and asked me how he could help.

When he asked me, "How can I help?" I initially snickered and thought to myself, *come on guy, I'm on your car lot looking at a $70,000.00 car, and you're going to ask me how you can help me?*

I thought to myself quickly, *there it is again, most PEOPLE REALLY DON'T THINK!*

That Salesman Was Truly Demonstrating That In That Moment.

I asked him if he had the keys for this car, and if I could look inside. He got the keys and opened the door, and as I sat down in the car, I was really absorbing every little detail of the interior. I was feeling like it belonged to me already, that I already owned it, and was driving it down the street. I looked that entire car over from top to bottom and front to back. I sat inside for about 5 minutes or so when the salesman made a comment, "You know, you can drive out of here in this car today." It was like he woke me up from a dream. I turned toward him as I was stepping out of the car and said, "Oh, I WILL BE BUYING ONE OF THESE! It's not going to be today but, I WILL BE BUYING ONE SOON."

And guess what? Exactly one month later I was at a different dealership, signing the papers and driving away in a BRAND-NEW SILVER 2009 CORVETTE!

So there it was. I had deliberately put the Laws to work for myself and the UNIVERSE brought it right to me. I was so excited!

Up until that point, I had never driven a car like that, let alone owned one. I was so blown away with how easy it had all come about, and how everything just fell right into place for me. It was like it was meant to happen.

AND GUESS WHAT? IT WAS!

Chapter 13

HOW THE HARLEY
CAME ABOUT

After owning the Corvette for 6 months or so, I decided to do the same thing and acquire a Harley Davidson for myself. I really had no intention of just running out and buying one; I just wanted to see how it was all going to play out. So I put it into my mind how nice it would be to have a new Harley.

It's mid 2009, and I had been riding motorcycles for the majority of my life. I had a nice motorcycle. (It wasn't a Harley, but it was nice.)

At the time, I used to ride with a lot of friends on weekends, taking all kinds of little different journeys.

One day, a friend who owned a Harley called on the phone and asked if I wanted to ride out with him to the Harley dealership to pick up a part for his bike. I decided to make the trip with him, and I was so glad that I did.

When we arrived at the dealership, my buddy went to the counter to get his part. I started walking the showroom floor looking at all the bikes on display. After checking them all out, I found myself standing next to and admiring what I considered to be the nicest bike on the showroom floor. I was all alone and I said to myself "NOW THAT IS A REALLY NICE BIKE!"

A few minutes later, I walked outside and was waiting for my friend, when he walked out talking to another guy that I had never met.

I came to find out, my buddy knew this guy. He was the son of one of the owners. My friend introduced me, and the guy handed me his card and told me if I was ever interested in a new bike that he would work me a deal because I was a friend of Dave.

About 3 weeks later I decided to give this guy a call and see what he could do for me.

I was very specific about what I wanted. I told him the style, color, I wanted these specific exhaust pipes installed on it, etc., and told him that if he could make it happen to give me a call back and we would talk.

He called me back about 3 days later and said that he thought he had the bike I was looking for at his dealership, all except for the exhaust pipes I wanted, which could be added later after he ordered them. I told the guy I did not want to mess around. If he could help me, I wanted to do everything over the phone and just walk in and sign the paperwork and drive away. He said that he understood, and we made arrangements to meet at his dealership.

When I arrived at the dealership, he met me out front. I asked him if he happened to have a different bike in the shop that had the exhaust pipes that I wanted on mine; I wanted to hear what they sounded like. He said he wasn't sure, and that he would go check.

As we walked the showroom floor looking at all the bikes, it didn't seem that there was a bike there with the same pipes.

We ended up standing next to the SAME BIKE that I had admired a few weeks back when I was at the store with my buddy. Out of curiosity, I looked at him and asked what was the price on this bike. I told him that if there was not much difference, I might be willing to just buy this bike, rather than investing in upgrades on the other bike anyway.

This particular bike had a bigger motor and a $10,000.00 chrome package, as well as many other extras. He went to check on the price, and came back a few minutes later telling me that the bike was only $5,000.00 more than the one I had gone there to purchase. When he said it, I decided on the spot to buy this one instead.

He quickly took care of all the details and paperwork, and I rode out of that place on what I considered to be one of the finest motorcycles I had ever seen.

And once again, everything that I had studied and applied had come right into play for me.

I got exactly what I wanted and in a very short amount of time.

But it didn't stop there!

Chapter 14

HOW I MET THE LOVE OF MY LIFE AND BEST FRIEND

By now it's early 2010, and a lot of great things had been happening for me in my life compared to where I was back between 2004 through 2006.

I knew that these teachings and the application of these principles were the cause for these good things happening in my life.

I mean, all I had done was change the way I looked at things, started believing and understanding this information, and giving the things that I desired attention. As I did, things had really changed drastically for me.

At the time, I was living with a friend splitting the rent on a house. Things were going great. I had my brand-new Corvette, my brand-new Harley Davidson, and my divorce had been finalized for almost 3 years. But something was still missing.

I was out on the front porch one night by myself just kicking back when all of a sudden I had this thought that I really wanted to find a woman who understood who I really was, a person who I could really open up and talk to, and at the same time, have some fun and enjoy my life with. At the time, I really didn't care about any specifics of who that person would be, other than the fact I wanted to make sure that person was totally committed to me and moving in the same direction that I was.

She had to be fun and have a great sense of humor. I told myself it would be great if she was spontaneous like me, and was willing to pick up and go on the spur of the moment like I was.

Well, the strangest thing happened. I was hanging out at the house one evening about two months later when my phone rang. It was a buddy of mine that I had been really close friends with, and had known since junior high school. We had played little league together, and were on the same high school baseball team as well.

It was 2010 and we had been out of high school for close to 30 years. Once we left high school, we both went our own ways and had lost contact with each other. I had gone into the military, had been married, and was now divorced for about 3 years.

When he called, I was totally blown away hearing from him after all this time. I quickly found out that he was living about 15 minutes from where I currently lived, which came as a surprise. When I asked him what he was doing, he told me that he was up at his sister's house helping her move and explained she had just gone through a divorce. Now, I knew that he had a couple of sisters because I had gone to school with one of them, but I had never met the particular sister that he was talking about.

So, when he told me that he was helping his sister who had just gone through a divorce, I said to him in a joking manner, "You know I'm divorced, knucklehead. Why don't you introduce me to your sister?" We laughed, and that was the end of the conversation about his sister.

We stayed on the phone and talked for a while longer catching up, and exchanged phone numbers. We agreed that we would stay in touch, and that we would get together soon, being that we lived so close to one another.

About 2 weeks later, my phone rang again. Guess who it was? Yep, it was my buddy from school. This time he asked me if I was serious about meeting his sister. I said I would love to. That's when he immediately handed the phone to his sister, and we started talking. Within a few minutes we had made arrangements for me to pick her up for dinner, and that was that.

We went out to dinner, and got along great. We decided to start spending more time together, having fun, and enjoying time together. One thing led to another, and we ultimately ended up moving in together.

We have been together for over 10 years now, and we are very happy together.

I was the only person who knew I wanted a good woman in my life, and Once Again The Universe Had Brought Me Exactly What I Had Asked For!

Chapter 15

OUR LIVES TOGETHER STARTED TO CHANGE

When all this came about, some really cool things started happening quickly.

You see, she was divorced and had a settlement that entitled her to a certain amount of dollars and the home she lived in during her previous 10-year marriage. Her ex-husband was now living in that home with his new girlfriend, and had no intention of leaving.

He knew that the property had been awarded to his ex-wife in the divorce, but he had no intention of honoring the court judgment.

So here she was with a court judgment entitling her to the property, but her ex-husband was not abiding by the law and the judgment that she was awarded from their divorce, and she couldn't force him to leave the home.

Needless to say, she wasn't happy being treated that way, and she didn't have any idea how she was going to get hold of the assets that she was entitled to.

I remember sitting out on the front porch with her one night as she expressed her concerns. After watching her cry about the situation and listening to what she was saying, I told her not to worry and that everything would work itself out.

About 2 weeks later I took a ride on my motorcycle to her sister's house, which was about 15-20 minutes from where we were currently living. As I was leaving, her husband came out and began to talk to me about what was taking place with my girlfriend and the home she was entitled to. You see, he knew her ex-husband pretty well. I had told him that we were planning to get everything that she was entitled to.

He proceeded to tell me that there was no way this guy was going to give her what she wanted. He went on to tell me that he knew this guy very well, and that he knew there was no way she was going to get anything from him.

I didn't really pay much attention to what he was saying because I knew that anything was possible. I listened to what he had to say, but when he was done, I told him that I wasn't sure how, but that my girlfriend's ex-husband was going give her everything she had been awarded in their divorce.

And guess what happened?

A few months went by, then the day came when I ended up introducing my girlfriend to an attorney friend of mine who ultimately decided to handle the case she had with her ex-husband.

Over the course of the next 4 months or so, he was able to recover everything she was entitled to legally. We ended up moving into the property that she acquired through her divorce.

The property was on close to an acre of land, and in a prime location. The back yard was about 1/2 acre separated by a fence, and was being used to store supplies from the business they previously had together.

The first thing we did was clean up the lot with the help of a few friends. Next, we measured the lot and put an ad in the local paper advertising it for rent. We figured that we would try to generate some income from the lot, being that it was just sitting there unused. So that's exactly what we did.

The very next day after running the newspaper ad, we were contacted by a local man who had a car transporting business and was looking for a place that he could set up a mobile office and park his trucks at night. We met with him over the next few days, and ultimately rented the yard out to him for his business. It was a win-win for both of us.

Chapter 16

HOW WE ENDED UP MOVING TO WASHINGTON

Shortly after he moved his business into the back lot, we were talking, and he mentioned how nice it was to have his business and trucks all in one place. He asked how long we had lived there, and wondered if we had ever thought about selling. I explained that we had no plans of selling or moving. He asked if he could be the first person notified if we ever did decide to sell the property. I laughed and said sure, but told him honestly that we really had no intentions of selling or moving.

I explained that the property was just going to be rental income for us. He was a pretty persistent guy. He continued making comments about how perfect the property was for his business, and proceeded to make it very clear that he wanted to be notified if we ever decided to sell. I laughed again and told him that IF we ever decide to sell, he would be the first to know.

We lived in that home for close to 2 years when one day, I came home frustrated with all the nonsense I was having to deal with at work. I pulled in the driveway and without even thinking, I picked up my phone and called my brother-in-law in Washington. He had been trying to get me to move up there from California for about 10 years, but I had never considered taking him up on the idea.

I told him that I had enough of California, and was seriously considering moving. I asked if I could come up and check the area out where he lived and visit for a few days. I explained that I would be bringing my girlfriend with me. He was pretty excited that I was considering the move. I made all the arrangements without her even knowing any of this.

When I approached her and asked if she wanted to go to Washington for 5 days to check out the area, she was all for it. So that's exactly what we did. We caught a flight, rented a car, and spent the next 5 days checking out the area in Washington where my brother-in-law lived. We had a great time while we were there.

This was in March of 2015.

When we got home, we returned to our normal routines.

After about 3 weeks of being back in California, I came home one day from work and asked my girlfriend what she thought about Washington, in terms of possibly living there. I was explaining that I was thinking possibly about moving to Washington, and was wondering how she would feel about moving there with me. She said she would be willing to go if that's what I wanted to do. She said she thought it would be exciting and fun.

We found a local realtor in the Washington area and began searching for homes that we liked in the areas surrounding where my brother-in-law lived.

We found about 7 or 8 places, and in May of 2015, we decided to go back up to Washington and physically look at those properties with the realtor. We looked at all of the properties on our list while we were there during that 3-day weekend.

After looking at the 8th property, we decided to make an offer on it. Our offer was initially turned down, but they did counteroffer with a price that we thought would work for us, so we agreed.

So here we were. We had made an offer on a property in Washington that was accepted, all contingent on our house in California selling. We did not have it listed at the time.

This is how perfectly all this worked for us: when we got home, I was ready to contact a local realtor and put our place on the market. Then I remembered that the guy who I rented our lot to wanted to be notified if we ever decided to sell the place.

That was a few years prior, so I wasn't really sure if he was still interested in buying the house.

When I saw him come back to his office, I decided to talk to him about possibly selling him the place, and seeing if he was still interested. To make a long story short, he committed to purchasing the house on the spot and the rest was history. We did everything on a handshake and in August of 2015, we finalized the deal and moved to our new place in Washington.

From the time we started TALKING about going to Washington and checking the area out, making the move and actually being in Washington in our new home together, only about 5 months had passed.

And Once Again, There It Was Right In Front Of Our Eyes. These Thoughts Had Turned Into Things!

Chapter 17

HOW WE FOUND
OUR BUSINESS

When we were in California, we had no idea what we were going to do for a living when we got to Washington. With the sale of our property, we had the finances to lay back for about 2 years without doing anything, but we did not want to do that. We had talked about trying to find a business that we could both work at together, but realized that we were going to do our research before we could really get serious about the idea.

So that's what we did. We started taking drives and becoming familiar with all the surrounding areas and communities. We were actively looking for local businesses for sale on the internet and talking to anyone we came in contact with, letting them know we were actively looking for business opportunities. However, we weren't finding many opportunities that we were interested in.

We had been at it for almost a year when I specifically remember my girlfriend telling me one day that she had the feeling we were eventually going to find the business we were looking for.

About 2 months later, she showed me an ad in the local newspaper from the town we were living in that said there was a 35-year-old local business for sale. The ad didn't elaborate on the nature of the business, but it gave the seller's contact information. After seeing the ad that morning, I said to her, "Why don't you give that person a call and set an appointment where we can sit down and talk?"

The business had been around for about 35 years but had an absentee owner, and in this community, that was not flying too well; the business was in a major decline. We called and made an appointment to meet with the owner at a local coffee shop.

We really had no idea what the business was all about or where it was actually located. After meeting with the owner, we wanted to go by and check the place out to see if it was worth us spending any more time or effort considering.

He told us where it was located, and asked that we NOT let his workers know that we were there as potential buyers. We agreed, and proceeded to go check the place out.

As soon as we arrived, we noticed that the place was definitely in a major decline. There were a couple of people working there who seemed as if they really didn't care too much about the place. We walked around looking at the place, and told the people working there that we were just in the area driving by and stopped in just to see what it was all about.

When we left, we were pretty excited about what we had seen. We had seen a lot of potential in the business, and had a lot of different ideas about changes we could make to improve the company. We knew in our hearts that if we worked together, we could make the business thrive. She had been part owner of a multi-million-dollar business with her ex-husband together for 10 years when they were married, and I had been running multi-million-dollar food manufacturing facilities for quite some time.

We talked about it for about a week or so, and decided to give the guy a call back and meet with him again.

This time, we had him come out to our house where we could relax and speak to him without being bothered by anyone. We asked him a lot of detailed questions about the business and what price he was hoping to sell it for. We asked if he could show us the past couple of years' financial statements to see where the business was financially. He had told us one thing about the state of the business, but the financials were telling a totally different story.

After we spent some time stewing on the opportunity (roughly another week), we decided to make contact with him once again to make him an offer based on what we thought it was currently worth, and what we were going to have to do to get the business up to where we wanted it to be. That price was about 1/3 of what he initially asked for, and we just weren't sure if he was willing to accept that offer; we figured it couldn't hurt to ask.

And guess what?

He thought about what we were offering and why, and ended up accepting our offer. We bought the business at an extreme discount, and have turned it into quite a nice little profit-maker.

The points that I want to make you aware of are, first, we were not from this community, and we had not lived in the area long. Second, we did not know anyone other than my brother-in-law. And third, we had NO idea how we were going to make this happen.

What happened was really unexplainable from many people's perspectives, but WE KNOW exactly HOW and WHY it all came about the way that it did!

THE PRINCIPLES AND LAWS OF THE UNIVERSE ONCE AGAIN WORKED FOR US, BRINGING US THIS BUSINESS!

JUST LIKE MAGIC!!!

Chapter 18

IT'S ALL IN AWARENESS

At this point, I want to make sure that you understand that I am in no way trying to brag or boast about all these great things that have taken place in our lives since I started learning and applying this information.

I've thought long and hard trying to figure out how I could really get you to understand that you really can have ANY-THING and EVERYTHING that you want. I finally came to the conclusion that the best way for me to help you understand and prove that all this information is really TRUE is to use my personal experiences as the rock-solid proof.

I know that there are a lot of you out there right now looking for this information, just like I was when it showed up in my life. So, I decided to sit down and write all this down and share it with YOU.

You see, YOU deserve nothing but the best, and it really is all out there for you. All you have to do is buy into all this stuff and amazing things that you never thought were possible will start taking place in your life, just like they have in ours.

You were born with the same tools that ALL of our great leaders were born with. You have exactly what you need to make it happen for yourself right now. You have probably just not been aware of it until now.

So, by now I have the full confidence that I've really got you THINKING!

You may remember when we first started that I said my goal and main purpose was to increase your AWARENESS so that you could create ANYTHING and EVERYTHING that your heart desires for the rest of your life.

If you're anything like me, or if this is your first time hearing about all this information, I'm sure there have been many times when it seemed like a light bulb turned on, and in the next minute you have possibly wondered and asked yourself, "Can all this really be TRUE?"

If that has happened to you, just remember that it is totally normal. It is only your Paradigm (which is YOUR PROGRAM) trying to keep you right where you are.

Don't worry about any of that. Know that it's there and understand what it is, but DO NOT let it stop you from moving forward.

Make the decision and tell yourself that you've been here long enough and it's not working, so it's time to try something different.

Understand that when you do something different, YOU are going to get different results. That's the ONLY thing that can happen!

Understand that you have made it this far because you have been looking for this information for a long time, and it has been brought here just for you.

Once again, it is NOT a coincidence that this book has found its way into your hands. It is here for a REASON.

IT ALL STARTS WITH AWARENESS!

And that's exactly what's happening. You are being made aware of something that deep down you have always known but never knew how to make it all happen because we were never taught the TRUTH.

"It's ALL IN AWARENESS"

There is a marvelous inner world that exists within man, and that revelation of such a world enables man to do, to attain, and to achieve ANYTHING he desires within the bounds or limits of nature.

At this point, I have explained several situations to you that I have personally experienced from understanding this information, processes, and teachings, and have created some pretty awesome things in my life. YOU have the ability to use this same information as well.

It doesn't matter what you want. It can be used for health, wealth, relationships, or any material things that you might want in your life.

The bottom line is this: if you keep doing what you've been doing, you're going to keep getting what you've been getting.

In order for you to change things, YOU HAVE TO CHANGE. And that change has to start with the way you THINK!

The thing that makes it so difficult is a lack of **BELIEF** that it could actually happen for you.

You have to understand that when you make a DECISION that YOU WANT SOMETHING, it is already yours. It does not matter what anyone else says or believes.

When you make that DECISION, you have to EXPECT it to show up!

Let me explain.

If you walk in the house and grab the remote control, point it at the TV, and hit the power button, you EXPECT the TV to turn on, RIGHT? And it does!

Now, let's say you want to watch a particular TV program on channel 55. You press 55 and hit enter, you EXPECT the TV to change channels and that program to be on the screen, RIGHT? And it does, again!

Your Mind Works The Same Way!

So, the question is really this: do YOU understand and realize that He ONLY delivers to FAITH Street?

The problem is that most of us stroll away from FAITH Street and get stuck over on I DON'T SEE HOW Circle. (He does not deliver there).

Instead of being stuck on FAITH Street, we step off onto I DON'T BELIEVE IT Boulevard, or IT TOOK TOO LONG Avenue.

Then, when He delivers to us on FAITH Street, it's just like the Post Office or FedEx—if we are not there to RECEIVE IT, it will be sent back!

YOU HAVE TO STAY ON FAITH STREET!

You can stay on FAITH Street by understanding who YOU really are, and understanding how these UNIVERSAL LAWS work. **THEY DO NOT CHANGE!**

Chapter 19

THE PHONE CALL
I WILL NEVER FORGET!

In Late September of 2019, my girlfriend received a phone call from her sister in California. The phone was on speaker so I could hear the conversation. My sister-in-law's daughter has 2 sons. They were living in Washington and had been bouncing from hotel to hotel for about 6 months.

My sister-in-law was pretty upset finding out that her grandsons were living this way. I heard her say to her sister that she was going to come to Washington before Christmas to find a place for her grandsons to live that would give them the stability she wanted for them.

Now, let me make sure you totally understand this situation. This lady is NOT a resident of Washington. Does NOT know the area. Does NOT have a car. And does NOT have any money. Yet she's saying that she is going to travel 1200 miles and find a house for her grandkids before Christmas, and create a solid living environment for them.

When they hung up the phone, we sat there and talked about the conversation that had just taken place. We both understand that NOTHING IS IMPOSSIBLE, so we decided to just sit back and see how this all was going to play out.

What took place over the course of the next few months was nothing short of amazing!

Within 1 week after that conversation, she called back and said that she had a flight scheduled to come to Washington.

Just as she said she would, she had somehow found a way to get to Washington. When the day arrived of the actual flight, we picked her up at the airport and let her stay with us while she was handling what she needed to handle.

I don't have any idea how she was capable of getting around to where she needed to go or meeting the people that she needed to meet with who could help her accomplish what she had set out to accomplish.

As I mentioned, she didn't have a car, she was not a resident of Washington, and as far as I knew, she didn't have any money. And she surely was not familiar with the area.

Heck, this was the first time she had been to Washington, so I know she didn't know anyone that she could call for help.

We had an obligation to our business, so we had to leave her every morning to go take care of our work and the community that we serve.

All I can tell you is that this lady somehow, before Christmas of that year, had her daughter and those 2 boys out of hotels and living in a house, just like she had said she was going to do!

Heck, she didn't just have her grandkids living in a house before Christmas, she had actually found a way to have the place decorated and furnished as well!

You should have seen the faces on her daughter and those 2 boys when their grandma told them that they were going to be moving into a house before Christmas. They lit up like a candle, and were so happy, as I am sure you can imagine.

The only thing I can say is that ALL the appropriate people, circumstances, and events that were necessary for her dream to come true were placed directly into her path to make it happen easily.

It was really awesome to stand back and watch all this take place. I was so happy for her and those kids. I knew exactly how and why all this had happened for her and those kids.

So, when it was all said and done, and after standing back and watching all this take place, I had a conversation with my sister-in-law about everything. I wanted her to realize what she had done. And I really wanted to point out to her that she had done this with her thoughts.

I asked her, "Do YOU realize what you just did?" I back-tracked with her from the initial phone call with her sister, and pointed out to her everything that had taken place over the last few months since.

I went on trying to explain to her how powerful her thoughts and words were. I was trying to open her up to the fact that she had all the POWER to make ANYTHING happen for herself that she wanted, for the rest of her life!

Believe it or not, even though she was aware of what she had accomplished in a short amount of time for her grandkids with the home, she had NO explanation as to how that all happened. She was NOT convinced that it applied to ANYTHING and EVERYTHING that she wanted. And she definitely did NOT believe she could do it anytime she wanted!

I was totally blown away that even after she had accomplished what she had accomplished, she still DID NOT BELIEVE in these LAWS and processes!

BUT THE FACT IS, SHE DID MAKE ALL THIS HAPPEN, AND IT ALL STARTED WITH HER THOUGHTS!

Chapter 20

HOW $62,000 SHOWED UP IN OUR BUSINESS ACCOUNT

In the early part of 2020, we decided that we wanted to see if we could take out a loan for our business in order to upgrade our cooler and purchase more inventory for our store.

We were thinking that about $30,000-$40,000 would be a good amount for us. We made contact with several lenders that were all willing to loan us the funds we wanted. However, we didn't like the terms and the costs of those loans, so we decided to hold off and wait to see what happened.

About 6 months passed and the COVID Virus was in full stream. At the time, our business CPA made contact with us and said that the government was going to be initiating some different programs geared toward helping small businesses, and that they would keep us posted on those programs as time went by.

About 6 weeks passed when we received an email detailing the various programs that were going to be offered by the government. One of them was the EIDL program. We had already known from talking to our CPA that this was going to be the program we were going to be interested in IF and when it became available.

About a week or so later, we received another email explaining more details about the programs, and asking which program we would be interested in. We clicked a button that was specific to the EIDL program, and immediately received an automated message on the screen that said, "THANK YOU for your interest," and letting us know that there had been millions of applicants. We would be notified later with further instructions.

About 6 weeks went by and we had not heard anything, so we decided to google "status of EIDL loan programs" to see if we could learn more about what was taking place.

What we found out was that once the initial interest and application was accepted, it would take between 2 and 4 months before we would receive instructions for the next step (whatever that would be).

Within 1 week we received another email confirming our interest in the EIDL loan, stating that the next email would have instruction and a link for us to follow. From that point, it should have taken 4-6 weeks, but we received the email within 2 weeks. We followed the instructions through the portal window and answered a few basic questions, which took only a few minutes.

Once the questions were answered and submitted, it stated that we would receive another notification within 4-6 weeks, IF we had been approved for this program.

Then something amazing happened!

Within 48 hours after submitting the questions, we were starting our business up for the day and we discovered that $62,000 had been deposited in our business account.

Initially, we really weren't sure where those funds had come from. We knew that we had answered a few questions to see if we qualified for this EIDL loan being offered to small businesses, but none of the paperwork that we had submitted ever mentioned an amount to be loaned. And they said that it would be 4-6 weeks before we would hear anything back one way or the other.

So you can imagine how shocked we were to find that $62,000 had been deposited in our business account.

We really had NO idea where it came from! We didn't know if it was an error through our bank or what was going on, so we notified our bank to see if they could help us figure it out. That's when we found out that our loan was approved through the EIDL program, and the amount of $62,000 had been deposited into our account.

We were totally blown away when we found this out because we not only received more than we were initially looking to borrow, but it also had a very low interest rate and the loan would not require any payments for a full year. It just seemed to keep getting better and better.

The point I want to make here is YES we did initially take a few steps toward the EIDL loan, but we literally had very little to do with it from our side.

The ONLY Explanation For This Event Is That The UNIVERSE Brought This Into Our Path!

Chapter 21

AS A MAN THINKETH

James Allen wrote a beautiful little book called *AS A MAN THINKETH*.

At the back of that book there is an area titled "Visions and Ideals." I would like to point out some areas that he touches on that I really believe are of vital importance for you to understand. They will surely help you to find your way to anywhere you want to go, IF YOU will just UNDERSTAND and BELIEVE.

He says, **The DREAMERS** are the saviors of the world!

Here are some portions of the book that I want to stress:

"As the VISIBLE world is sustained by the INVISIBLE, men, through their trials and sins and sordid vocations, are nourished by the **BEAUTIFUL VISIONS** of their solitary DREAMERS, The world cannot forget its DREAMERS, **it cannot let their IDEALS fade and die;** it lives in them; it knows them as the **REALITIES which it SHALL** one day see and know. He who cherishes a beautiful vision, a lofty ideal in his heart, **WILL one day REALIZE it.**"

"We have to Cherish OUR Visions; Cherish OUR ideals; Cherish the music that stirs in OUR heart and the beauty that forms in OUR MINDS. For out of them **WILL grow ALL delightful conditions**."

"DREAM lofty DREAMS, and as YOU DREAM, YOU WILL become! Your **VISION is the PROMISE** of what **YOU SHALL one day be**."

"YOUR DREAMS are the seedlings of **YOUR REALITIES**."

"YOU can NOT travel WITHIN and stand still WITHOUT."

"YOU will fall, remain or rise with YOUR THOUGHTS, YOUR VISION, YOUR IDEAL."

"YOUR VISION that you glorify in **YOUR MIND**, the IDEAL that you hold in your HEART, This YOU will build your life by, **THIS YOU WILL BECOME**!"

In other words, we have to **BELIEVE in our dreams**; we have to see them in our MINDS and give them the attention that they deserve just like we would with a garden. We have to hold them close to our hearts and **NEVER** give up on them.

FOR SURELY IT WILL COME. IT IS LAW!

Something To Remember:

Spirit just IS.

It is 100% evenly present at the same time.

WE are Spiritual Beings, and we live in a Physical Body.

Spirit ALWAYS manifests through its polar opposite. That is what prayer is.

Prayer is the movement that takes place through SPIRIT and forms with and through US!

Most people are praying for things that they don't want.

We have an intellect, and our emotional state is dictated by how we use it. It's with our intellect that we make choices.

It's with the intellect that we create the IDEA that we impress on our emotional mind.

That is what is manifested through the body.

Spirit operates according to LAWS. One of those LAWS is the LAW OF VIBRATION!

The Spiritual side of us is the HIGHEST and the Physical side is the LOWEST.

The Spirit ALWAYS manifests through the PHYSICAL.

You may be wondering how it does that. It all depends on how we THINK!

That's what all our great leaders throughout history have all agreed on. WE BECOME WHAT WE THINK ABOUT.

So, we use our thoughts and build the IDEA in our MIND. We HOLD that thought on the screen of our mind. IF we hold that thought long enough, IT WILL MANIFEST with and through us because we are instruments of the SPIRIT!

Chapter 22

HOW I HAVE USED THESE PRINCIPLES WITH WEIGHT LOSS

In February of 2020, I was at home, and for some strange reason I jumped on the scale in the bathroom and discovered that I weighed 253 lbs. I was literally shocked. I actually had to look at it a second time to make sure I was actually seeing what I was seeing on the display. When I got off that scale, I could not believe that I had somehow gained so much weight. I had never weighed that much in my life.

Initially, in my mind standing there by myself, I said, "Oh no, this is not going to happen with me. I'm going to take care of this situation and get myself down to where I want to be, starting now."

I didn't say one word about how much I weighed to anyone.

The next thing I know, within a few days of my weight discovery, I overheard my brother-in-law and his sister having a conversation about losing weight and possibly going on a diet.

When I heard what they were talking about, I decided to get involved in the conversation and let them know that I also wanted to lose some weight, and that I wanted to start as soon as possible. I had never been in this position before, and I wasn't sure exactly what they had planned or if they were just talking, so I decided that I was going to initiate a few things on my own right away.

I decided I was going to start walking between 1 and 2 miles a day each morning, start drinking more water, and paying closer attention to what and when I was eating.

When I began to pay attention, I realized that I had not been drinking enough water. I used to drink a lot of water, but had somehow gotten away from the habit. The only walking I had been doing was in my day-to-day operations at our store, and doing yard work on the weekends. I also noticed that I had really let my eating habits decline as well.

When I would sit down for dinner, I would eat till I was stuffed. It had become a ritual for me to make a pit stop in the kitchen have a glass of milk along with 4-6 cookies as I was on my way to bed. Oh, and let's not even talk about the giant bowls of ice cream that I would eat while watching TV at night.

As you can see, I had really let things get away from me without even paying attention to what I was doing.

I am not going to say that it was not tough initially to make these changes for myself, because it was.

You see, anytime you decide to make a change for whatever reason, it requires you to change your current habits. The habits that I had put in place for myself over time without paying attention had gotten me to this extra weight.

So, the first thing that I did was make a decision for MYSELF that I was going to set a GOAL of getting my weight down to between 190-200 lbs, which is about where I thought I should be for my height.

That would mean that I was setting out to lose between 53 and 63 lbs, and I wanted to accomplish that by the end of the year.

I really had no idea how I was going to accomplish this goal, and I sure did not know how I was going to do it in the time-frame I had set for myself.

There were all these crazy voices going on inside my head that were all telling me why I could not do it, and believe me, for about 2 weeks every night on the way to bed a voice was telling me not to forget the milk and cookies.

Well, by initiating the walking and initially changing my eating habits to smaller portions, getting away from the ice cream, milk, and cookies, and drinking more water, I am proud to say that 6 months later I was weighing in at 210 lbs. That's a loss of 43 lbs in 6 months. I had no doubt that by the end of the year I would be at my target weight of 190-200 lbs.

I hear people talking all the time about buying diet pills and going on fancy diets. I really don't think all that is necessary. I have come to the conclusion and really believe that it's just like anything else.

IT ALL STARTS WITH YOUR THOUGHTS!!

Steve Jobs said it so well:

He said, "YOU can't connect the dots looking forward. You can ONLY connect them looking backward!"

So, YOU have to TRUST that somehow those dots will connect in the FUTURE.

That means that you are always going to be walking into the dark. You're going to be walking into an area that you have never been to before.

You can take that as a scary thing, OR you can look at it as a magnificent opportunity! (Where EVERY DAY is an adventure.)

You can look at yourself and say THIS IS WHERE I AM. I know how I got here, and this is where I WANT to go.

The moment our BELIEFS MATCH with any state, WE FUSE with it.

This union results in the activation of its PLOTS, PLANS, CONDITIONS, and CIRCUMSTANCES.

At that point, everything changes. This new state of conscious awareness becomes our home from which we view the world.

IF we are observant, we will see reality shaping itself to the model of our IMAGINATION.

THIS IS ALL OUR IMAGINATION AT WORK!

WHEN you buy into it. All kinds of STRANGE THINGS WILL START TO HAPPEN. BUT YOU have to buy into it.

When YOU do, you can't see what has to happen, so YOU have to TRUST and BELIEVE!

You have to act like the person YOU want to become.

You have to realize that some of the people who are close to you are going to ask you why you are acting that way. They might even laugh at you, think you are crazy, or make fun of you.

YOU have to be strong enough to say, "TOO BAD. YOU don't really KNOW WHO I AM!"

Not many people can or will do that. It's NOT easy. That's why there are only about 3 people out of 100 who will do it.

But when YOU do, THE WAY JUST SUDDENLY HAPPENS!

Before you know it, YOU ARE THERE! (Right where you wanted to go.)

So don't try to connect the dots looking forward. It is NOT your job.

YOU just have to TRUST and BELIEVE that somehow the dots will connect in the future. BECAUSE THEY WILL!

Chapter 23

CHOICES AND DECISIONS

So now we are at the point where the rubber meets the road.

As I have already mentioned, YOU have the ability to make your own choices and your own decisions.

That means that right now, YOU have the ability to grab onto this information and use it to the best of your ability and apply it in your life to create ANYTHING and EVERYTHING that you can possibly want for the rest of your life; OR you can continue to do what you have been doing and NOT BELIEVE. If you choose the latter, YOU will be taking all this information and knowledge and throwing it right out the window.

THAT CHOICE IS YOURS!

This book has been written for YOU!

Hopefully by now YOU realize that this is ALL ABOUT YOU!

Since becoming aware of this information and applying it in my life for close to 15 years, then taking the opportunity to look back and see what it has done for me, I made the decision to become a personal mentor and help as many people as

I can create the lives of their dreams. I know that if I can do it, ANYONE can.

I want you to know up front I am very selective about who I choose to work with, but if you are **SERIOUS** about making great things happen for yourself starting now, are willing to make a **COMMITTED DECISION** to yourself, are ready and willing to follow some simple instructions and spend at least **1 hour a day on YOURSELF,** then I want to talk with you!

You can send an e-mail to Randy at yourpath2freedom1@gmail.com

My website is www.RandyJNoland.com

You can also contact me through my website if you would like.

Before reaching out to me, please take some time to THINK about what it is that you truly want in your life, and be sure to include those things in your email.

Remember, you can have ANYTHING and EVERYTHING YOU WANT!

NOTHING IS IMPOSSIBLE!

Just reach down inside and ask yourself what it is that YOU WANT. Don't ask anyone else. They do NOT know what YOU want OR who YOU really are.

So please DO NOT let ANYONE else control who YOU are OR where YOU WANT to go.

Once I receive your e-mail, I will respond and hopefully we can make some arrangements to talk and see if my coaching program is a good fit for both of us.

Remember, this is serious stuff. This is all about YOU and YOUR LIFE, and creating the life that YOU so much WANT and deserve!

I'm going to make a very bold statement here, and I'm going to let you know that I really don't care whether YOU BELIEVE it OR not. I hope that you do, but honestly, that is totally on you!

I already know and understand that this information is real, and that it does work IF you are willing to apply yourself and practice the things that are required to get the results you want!

So here goes,

IF YOU CAN TELL ME WHAT YOU WANT,
I CAN SHOW YOU HOW TO GET IT!!
GUARANTEED!!!
IT IS YOUR TIME! ARE YOU READY??

To YOUR FREEDOM and SUCCESS,
Randy

ABOUT THE AUTHOR

Hello,

My Name is Randy J Noland. I am 58 years old, and I currently reside in the town of East Wenatchee in the state of Washington.

I would like to start by letting you know that I am so happy that you have found your way here with me today.

It is NO coincidence that you have found your way here. YOU are here for a reason.

Before we talk about who I am and why we have arrived here together today, I think it is vitally important that you understand and realize that I am absolutely NO different than YOU are!

And WE are no different than any of our past great leaders, or anyone else for that matter.

We were all brought here with the same tools, and were built exactly the same way!

The only thing that separates you and me is our KNOWL-
EDGE and BELIEFS.

That is because most of us were never made aware or taught
any of the information that is available throughout this book.

(At least I know that I never was).

Which brings us to the point of why we have found ourselves
here together today.

YOU were brought here for a major eye-opener … a WAKE-
UP call!

Just like I was at the beginning of 2005.

You see, back in 2004, I was probably at the lowest point in my
life because of a decision that I made. That decision basically
caused me to lose everything I had. It left me with the clothes
on my back, $60 in my pocket, and my truck.

At the time, I thought my world had been turned completely
upside down. But in all reality, it had really been turned right
side up.

I just wasn't aware of it at the time.

Then one night in early 2005, right out of the blue, a man by
the name of Bob Proctor was brought into my life for the second time through a video that he was presenting that I somehow happened to stroll upon. That video and the things Bob
was talking about that night caught my attention and resonated
with me so much that it ended up taking hold of me like nothing I had ever experienced before in my life.

Believe me when I tell you things were not going well for me at the time. I was definitely not happy with what was going on in my life, to say the least. I was scared to death. I didn't know if I was going to be living out on the streets, or in the back of my truck. I felt like I had been backed up against a wall with nowhere to turn.

At the time, I had NO idea as to why this information that Bob was presenting that night took hold of me the way that it did, but I now realize that I had been looking for it for a long time and I definitely needed it to show up when it did!

And now, 15 years later, I can TRULY say that I am so glad that it showed up when it did.

It caused me to WAKE UP and seriously start PAYING ATTENTION!

It pushed me to start learning some things that I was not aware of at the time and had NEVER heard of OR been taught before.

I really found the information that he was teaching to be both fascinating and breath-taking at the time. And I still do to this day.

I am so happy and grateful that BOB and his teachings were brought into my life that night!

If it wasn't for this information, it's hard to say where I may have ended up.

Since that day, and for the last 15 years, I have been learning, studying, and applying the information that I learned and continue to learn through Bob and his mentors into my life. And because I made the decision to open myself up to some different things and apply those teachings and knowledge into my life, there have been some pretty amazing things that have resulted from it. Because of these results and experiences, I find it necessary to share this information with as many people as I can in the hopes of helping others do the same in their lives.

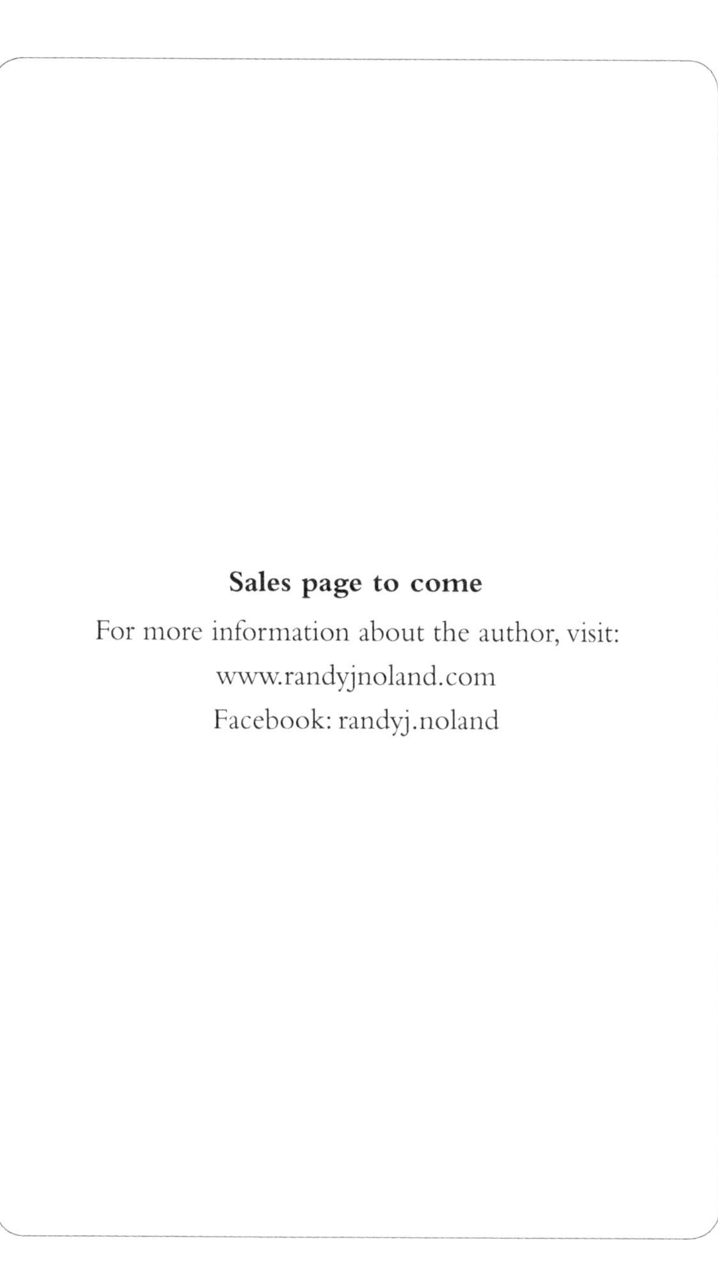

Sales page to come

For more information about the author, visit:

www.randyjnoland.com

Facebook: randyj.noland

With every donation, a voice will be given to
the creativity that lies within the hearts of
our children living with diverse challenges.

By making this difference, children that may
not have been given the opportunity to have their
Heart Heard will have the freedom to create
beautiful works of art and musical creations.

Donate by visiting

HeartstobeHeard.com

We thank you.

www.ingramcontent.com/pod-product-compliance
Lightning Source LLC
Chambersburg PA
CBHW060944050726
47592CB00003B/1099